W9-AWY-098

AN ELVIN MCDONALD GARDENING BOOK

THE FLOWER GARDENER'S ANSWER BOOK

THE FLOWER GARDENER'S ANSWER BOOK

by Francesca Morris

VNR VAN NOSTRAND REINHOLD COMPANY
New York Cincinnati Toronto London Melbourne

Copyright © 1978 by Francesca Morris
Library of Congress Catalog Card Number 78-7969
ISBN 0-442-80567-5 cloth
ISBN 0-442-80595-0 paper

All rights reserved. No part of this work covered by the copyright
hereon may be reproduced or used in any form or by any
means—graphic, electronic, or mechanical, including photocopying,
recording, taping, or information storage and retrieval
systems—without written permission of the publisher.

Printed in the United States of America

Published by Van Nostrand Reinhold Company
A division of Litton Educational Publishing, Inc.
135 West 50th Street, New York, NY 10020, U.S.A.

Van Nostrand Reinhold Limited
1410 Birchmount Road
Scarborough, Ontario M1P 2E7, Canada

Van Nostrand Reinhold Australia Pty. Ltd.
17 Queen Street
Mitcham, Victoria 3132, Australia

Van Nostrand Reinhold Company Limited
Molly Millars Lane
Wokingham, Berkshire, England

16 15 14 13 12 11 10 9 8 7 6 5 4 3 2 1

Library of Congress Cataloging in Publication Data
Morris, Francesca.
  The flower gardener's answer book.
  Includes index.
  1. Flower gardening—Miscellanea.   2. Plants,
Ornamental—Miscellanea.   I. Title.
SB405.M74 1978   635.9   78-7969
ISBN 0-442-80567-5
ISBN 0-442-80595-0 pbk.

To my friend, Elvin McDonald

Contents

Foreword

Although Francesca Morris and I have been good friends for many years, we didn't really get to know each other as gardeners until we worked together in compiling the 16-volume *Good Housekeeping Illustrated Encyclopedia of Gardening* (New York: Hearst Magazines Book Division, 1975). As the editor in chief, it didn't take me long to realize that Francesca was my staff member most likely to know the answers to difficult plant questions, especially when flowers were the subject.

In time, "Ask Francesca" became my byword and when our work was completed on the *Encyclopedia*, I suggested that she consider doing a book filled with practical, personable answers to all the most common and worrisome questions people ask about flowering plants. Francesca responded enthusiastically, as did the editors at Mason/Charter Publishers when I proposed the idea to them; and so, today you hold in your hands *The Flower Gardener's Answer Book*.

What is perhaps most important about Francesca as a garden writer is that virtually all of her information has been gained by first-hand experience, set within the framework of a busy life as a free-lance editor and writer, as the devoted mother of two children and the wife of composer John Morris. Although their primary residence—and garden—is in Westchester County, about an hour's drive north of New York City, John's career requires that they spend several months of the year in Hollywood and sometimes an equal amount of time in London. In addition, they have a house in Maine surrounded by low-upkeep perennial flowers and shrubs that don't mind the occasional salt spray from the Atlantic Ocean. Francesca's answers are thus based on what she has learned by gardening, both indoors and outdoors in extremely varied climates and circumstances. I recommend that first you read her book from cover to cover, and then refer back to it for specific answers as the need arises.

Elvin McDonald
Editor in Chief
Popular Gardening Magazine

Preface

We Americans love our homes and hearths, and this love has spilled out of doors into our gardens. The explosion of gardening centers across the country attests to the joy more and more of us are deriving from gardening. No matter how much or how little outdoor space is available to us, we try to have something in bloom all through the growing season—whether it be the long gardening period of the southern states, or the shorter ones of the long-winter areas of the North. And indoors we grace our houses with blooming plants when we cannot garden al fresco.

To me, a great part of the charm of gardening is swapping plants with fellow gardeners. A walk around my garden comprises a tour of fondly remembered gardens of friends: those cheddar pinks from Jacqueline Heriteau Hunter's garden in Westport, Connecticut; the single-flowered summer chrysanthemums and feverfew from Dorothy Woodruff's perennial border at Pemaquid Point, Maine; the roses from Larry Power's Kent, Connecticut, garden. I could go on and on. Indoors, the house plants, well—suffice to say, many of them derive from Elvin McDonald's lavish and seemingly endless indoor displays.

But there's often a good deal of frustration built into those cherished plants. In the haste of digging or dividing them just before we're ready to head for home, we forget to observe where they are growing or ask how they thrive best. The generous host or hostess may think you know. The following year your new plant remains stubbornly flowerless or droops dejectedly.

The purpose of this book is to answer those questions you forget to ask. Because of space limitations, it is not all-inclusive but attempts to deal with some of the most frequently asked questions about some of the more commonly grown garden and house plants.

My thanks to all those people who helped me acquire knowledge, as well as plants, over the years: Jacqueline, Dorothy, Larry, and Elvin, and to Jeannette Lowe of Burpee's and Margaret Ohlander—not to mention the dedicated nursery people at garden centers in Westchester County and Maine. Special thanks to my supportive though long-suffering family—all, thank heaven, good cooks and great diggers: my husband, John, my son, Evan (and girlfriend, Jan) and my daughter, Bronwen.

Francesca Morris

Chappaqua, New York
May 1977

1

Basic Gardening 101

The object of this book is to help you coax your flowering plants into putting their best foot forward. Actually, the right plant in the right place with the right treatment will be only too happy to expend its energy and turn itself into a flowering showpiece. As you look up answers to problems similar to yours, you will find that the solutions usually lie in one of these areas: location (both geographic and in the confines of your own garden and house); soil condition; fertility; moisture (too much or too little); pruning (how and when); pests and diseases (avoiding same); and mulches (to complement all of the above).

These are the keystones to success with flowering—as well as all—plants. They are simple things, really, easily provided, but sometimes ignoring one or more of them will make the difference between success and failure.

But, as you read, you will find, too, that you may be growing some plants successfully although you may not be observing all the so-called rules. Gardening is full of such mysteries. As has often been said, it is not an exact science and we can only conclude that plants really have a will to thrive and flower, and often will adjust to the most adverse conditions.

Location: This is the first and foremost consideration to be given to anything you acquire for your garden—indoors or out. There is no point to planting a bougainvillea outdoors in Boston nor trying to raise a cyclamen in the 80° F.

temperature of an overheated apartment. The poor bougainvillea will die because it is not "hardy" in Boston winters. Hardiness refers to the amount of cold a garden plant will take. A bougainvillea is "tender." That is to say it is a plant which needs a relatively warm, frost-free temperature year round. Conversely, winter-hardy plants may not thrive in constant warmth because they need a period of cold in which to go dormant. These are geographic distinctions you need to consider before acquiring an outdoor plant.

The second consideration with reference to location, once you have established the suitability of a plant to your climate, is the actual positioning. Most blooming plants need sun—at least six hours of it—in order to flower, but others are at their best in "partial shade." Partial shade implies an eastern or western exposure, screened from hot, noonday sun. The screening can be supplied by a building or a tall tree or shrub, a lath house, an arbor, or anything that casts a shadow.

In addition to screening from too much sun, many flowering plants need protection from wind. We need to be wary of windswept sites where late winter or early spring cold winds can nip developing flower buds.

Soil Condition: What does soil condition mean? One phase of that question refers to the quality, the other to its acidity or alkalinity. First let's consider the quality of the soil. Good soil is one which is rich in organic content. Woods soil, where generations of trees have shed their leaves each fall so that the under layers decay is naturally rich, humusy soil.

There is no substitute for organic matter in the soil. Not only does it add fertility and supply trace elements, but the water-retention properties of organic matter has no manmade replacement. So soil building is one in which we emulate nature's lead and add decayed organic materials.

Good soil, then, means a rich crumbly humus-filled material. Most plants are at their best growing in such soil. Oddly enough, however, there are plants whose geographic origins make them happiest in poor, light soil. Again one must know individual plant needs.

Since most plants prefer a good humus-filled soil, let's concentrate first on how to achieve it. The world's best soil builder is manure. Unfortunately, today, for most of us, it is hard to come by. Commercially prepared dehydrated manure, though usable as a fertilizer, does not add humus to the soil. If you are lucky enough to have access to a neighbor's stable or barn (or, better yet, your own) it is well worth going to the trouble of retrieving it. Manure can also be bought by the truck load in most suburban and rural parts of the country.

You will note the term "well-rotted manure" occurs constantly throughout my book. Fresh manure will burn plant roots, so the manure will have to be heaped and allowed to age, just as compost is, until it looks like crumbly black soil.

Compost ranks next on the list of soil builders, and like manure, it is a time-honored garden standby. It should be used even if you do have manure because there are some plants—most notably bulbous ones—which object to close contact with manure. Compost can be had by anyone for the making. Since you can't be a gardener without some land, somewhere in even a small garden you should be able to find a spot where you can maintain a small compost heap. If your gardening is confined to a city terrace you can even make compost in a garbage pail. The compost materials are available to all since they are nothing more than layers of grass clippings, leaves, and waste vegetable matter, heaped up with a little soil.

An outdoor compost heap should not be in full sun nor heavy shade. It should be flat topped, or slightly concave so that it will trap water. The bottom layer of the heap should be branches or boughs which will allow air to circulate under the pile. A good size for a compost heap is about 4 feet wide, 4 feet high and as long as you like. But it can be any size you can conveniently fit in an out-of-the-way spot. Over the foundation of boughs, spread a layer up to 5 inches deep of leaves, grass, clippings, pine needles, wood chips, old mulch material such as sawdust and straw, old annuals pulled up in the fall and all the vegetable kitchen wastes such as potato peelings and carrot scrapings. Anything that was once a live plant can be used except diseased plant matter, large woody pieces which will take longer to decay, or large seeds (such as squash) that may germinate. If you have manure to spare, add a layer of that. Next, cover this vegetative debris with a thin layer of soil. Over this scatter wood ashes or ground limestone to counteract acidity. Continue to layer the pile, alternating 5 inches of vegetable material with a thin layer of soil. The bacterial action of microorganisms naturally present in the soil start the pile working. The pile will heat up causing the organic matter to decay more rapidly. A well-made compost heap will turn to finished compost in about three months.

If the content of the pile is largely leaves, add a high nitrogen fertilizer such as blood meal. If rock phosphate and bone meal are added, the finished compost will have all the necessary ingredients of a balanced fertilizer.

Wet the pile thoroughly and keep it moist—not sodden. In two or three weeks, turn the pile so the material at the outer edges is placed in the center. The center of the pile is where the heat is most intense so decomposition is quickest. Continue turning the pile every couple of weeks. New materials can be added to the center of the pile.

If you have room, you can make several compost piles, starting them a few weeks apart so you always have finished compost on hand. Incidentally, a properly handled compost heap does not have an offensive odor.

There are a number of devices on the market for tidily containing compost. Investigate them to see if one of them will facilitate your compost making. To make compost in a garbage pail, start with a foot or so of soil and dig in kitchen wastes and trimmings from terrace and house plants.

Failing access to compost or manure, baled sphagnum peat moss is an excellent soil builder and readily available everywhere. It does not add to the fertility of the soil, but it does improve its structure.

As important as the quality of the soil to a plant is its pH. This abbreviation means potential of hydrogen and is used to denote the acidity or alkalinity of the soil. It refers to the balance of hydrogen ions to those of hydroxyl ions. When these ions are in balance the soil is neutral and has a reading of 7.0 on a logarithmic scale running from 1 to 14. The numbers below 7.0 indicate acidity in the soil, those above indicate alkalinity.

Through much of the country soils are naturally slightly acid, but in some areas they are highly alkaline. Most plants tolerate slightly acid conditions, but all plants are sensitive to excesses in either direction. Those that are native to alkaline parts of the country will need to have the soil adapted to their needs.

A simple test with a piece of litmus paper purchased at the drug store will give you a clue as to which your soil is: if the paper on being pressed into moist soil turns pink, the soil is acid; if it turns blue, the soil is alkaline. Commercial soil-testing kits will give you a more sophisticated reading so that the actual degree of acidity or alkalinity can be determined. County extension agents, agricultural colleges, and botanical gardens all offer soil testing services. Get in touch with the source nearest you to find out the procedure and charges, if any. Samples should be taken from different parts of the garden as there may be variations on even a small property.

The pH of the soil can be changed by the addition of the appropriate materials. To make an alkaline soil more acid, use any of the following: shredded oak leaves, manure, peat moss, sawdust, tea leaves, coffee grounds, aluminum sulfate, sulfur, superphosphate. To make the soil more alkaline, add crushed limestone, wood ashes, marl, or bone meal.

Fertility: Soil rich in organic material has a certain amount of natural fertility. Manure has some fertility and, although the amount varies with the kind (poultry manure, for instance, is richer than cow manure), it is not enough to be sufficient in itself. Very well-made compost should be quite fertile.

Since the home gardener probably does not balance his compost materials scientifically, but rather uses what is at hand, a regular program of fertilizing should be followed. In gardening terms this is referred to as "feeding." For flowering plants in general (there are exceptions, such as roses, which are called "gross feeders" and need more feeding, and house plants whose roots are confined to a limited amount of soil) two minimum feedings are essential: one early in the season before the plant blooms and one immediately after blooming. Fertilizers should not be used after the midseason point, particularly in colder areas of the country in order to avoid stimulating tender young growth on the plant that will not be sturdy enough to survive freezing winter weather. In areas of the country where plants do not freeze, fertilizer should be withheld in order to give the plant a chance to rest.

The three fertilizing elements needed by growing things are nitrogen, phosphorus, and potassium. The chemical analysis which is symbolized by numbers on packaged fertilizers always read in that order; for instance, a 5-10-5 analysis stands for 5 percent nitrogen, 10 percent phosphorus, and 5 percent potassium. Nitrogen is probably the most essential of the three as it is needed for stem and foliar growth, lacking which there is no plant. Phosphorus is utilized by the plant to produce a healthy root system and to develop its fruits and seeds. To this end, it is most important to the production of flowers. A fertilizer with a high nitrogen analysis such as 10-5-5 is useful to the young plant in its formative stages, but when it reaches its blooming size, then it should be fed with fertilizer in which the second number (for phosphorus) is the largest. The third element, potassium or potash, also aids in strong root development and increases resistance to some diseases.

There are also a variety of trace elements, many of which are present in the soil and some in organic fertilizers. Most chemical fertilizers also usually include a variety of trace elements. Perhaps the most important of these is iron. However, in order for a plant to avail itself of the iron present in the soil or a fertilizer, there must be some acidity in the soil. Alkaline soil does not allow the iron to become soluble and so it cannot be taken up by the plant. This lack of iron is most pronounced in a variety of acid-loving plants such as rhododendron, camellia, citrus, and gardenia and results in a condition called "chlorosis" in which the leaves yellow although the ribs and veinings remain green. Incorporating acid fertilizers into the soil is the specific cure.

Chemical fertilizers are formulated with analyses correct for every need. Some are sold specifically for certain plants. In any case, a reading of the chemical analysis will tell you what the composition of a fertilizer is. Organic fertilizers usually do not have all three elements, and here again it is necessary to read the analysis which will appear on the package. Organic fertilizers that are easily purchased and are high in nitrogen are: cottonseed meal, dried blood, and fish meal. Organic materials high in phosphorus and easily available are bone meal and rock phosphate. Potash is found in wood ashes. Hardwood ash has a higher potash content than ashes from conifers.

For the new gardener who is all thumbs and all of them brown, the organic materials are safer to use simply because an accidental overdose will not result in injury to the plant. Chemical fertilizers must be used strictly according to package instructions as an overdose can severely burn plant roots (or leaves if it is accidentally dropped on them). Also, chemical fertilizers are more readily washed out of the soil by rain and watering. The newer slow-release chemical fertilizers are also safer to use and longer lasting.

It has been my experience that the organic fertilizers such as cottonseed meal are in somewhat shorter supply than the chemical ones and, if not bought early in the season, are hard to come by.

Moisture: Newly set plants always need careful watering, at least the first year until their roots are firmly established. Beyond that, some plants are at their best when soil is constantly moist. Then there are plants, of which cacti are the most obvious example, which can get along under drought conditions. As a general rule, though, no plant will last long if its roots are constantly sodden and waterlogged (except for bog and water plants). For almost all plants good drainage is necessary.

If your land is sodden and muddy even during dry periods, it obviously needs draining. Drainage can be

7

achieved by the expensive method of installing an underground system of tiles and gravel to carry off the excess water. For the small property, a simpler and attractive solution is to make raised beds. A retaining wall of some sort will be needed such as a low dry or mortared stone wall, one of brick or railroad ties. Before the soil is filled in, a layer of several inches of gravel or small stones should be spread so that the raised bed does not draw up excessive water from the wet ground below.

In very dry areas of the country, many gardens have built-in watering systems to facilitate the constant need for watering. In other parts of the country, during seasons of low rainfall, the gardener will need to water if a week goes by without rain, especially during hot weather. Sprinklers and canvas soakers (long hoselike canvas tubes through which the water seeps) are recommended as opposed to hand-held hoses or watering cans simply to insure an adequate amount of water is given. When watering any growing plant, from house plants to trees, it is essential to water thoroughly. Frequent shallow waterings cause plant roots to reach upward for moisture resulting in a shallow-rooted plant subject to being uprooted by winds and heaved by frosts. Deep watering will enable the roots to develop naturally downward, thus anchoring the plant.

When watering house plants, always water until moisture collects in the plant saucer. After an hour or so, empty off the excess to prevent the roots from becoming waterlogged. If the plants are set on trays of pebbles, it is relatively easy to dispose of this water as it can simply be poured off into the trays. Otherwise carry a bucket or bowl around to hold the surplus. In watering large plants which are difficult to lift, try to learn the amount of water the plant needs before it begins to engulf the saucer and always use that amount. In case you do unwittingly flood the saucer, a bulb baster from the kitchen is a handy way to extract the excess.

Both indoors and out, the ideal time to water is early in the day so that the plants have a chance to utilize the water during their hours of active photosynthesis. Morning watering also allows wet foliage to dry out in the sun, cutting down on the incidence of fungal diseases that thrive on wet, slowly drying foliage. Of course, if watering in the evening after work is the only possible time you can perform this chore, it is better to water then than allow the plants to wither. But be sure to avoid overhead watering late in the day.

Pruning: Some pruning of flowering plants is a must and is a subject which the timid gardener approaches with trepidation. Judicious pruning can stimulate much better flowering production on many plants. Pruning at the wrong time of year can result in no blossoms at all as the gardener may have pruned off all the buds before they had a chance to flower.

The specifics of pruning for flowering have been dealt with in the answers to questions. But it is a subject which the dedicated gardener should study in depth and I recommend a trip to the library to familiarize yourself with the books that are available on the subject.

In cutting any outdoor plant, whether actually pruning or merely removing dead flowers, always make cuts diagonally so that rainwater can run off. Water trapped on a stem can induce rotting.

Pests and Diseases: Here again is a subject too vast to be fully handled in a book of this size and the reader should consult a good garden encyclopedia. Some of the problems encountered in this area have been answered as they arose. One highly recommended solution to many plant diseases is to research information about a plant before buying it. Hybridizers' newer introductions are more and more frequently being bred for resistance to some of the noxious diseases to which specific plants are prone. Study new catalogs issued by major plant suppliers. Disease resistance is always noted. Try to buy these varieties.

Although you may be tempted, avoid buying bargain plant material. All too often such plants are selling at low prices because they are infected and reputable nurseries would not handle them. Examine plants carefully before buying them. If you touch a plant and clouds of whiteflies soar into the air, head for home without buying.

Healthy, well-fed, well-watered plants growing in good soil are your second best bet in avoiding pests and diseases. In a small garden, the occasional pest can be dealt with by hand picking or a diseased branch cut off and destroyed. But when a disease or an insect strikes in volume, a good garden center will have the appropriate antidote and be able to advise you on its use. Also, county extension agents in your area will be familiar with the troubles that are common where you are and will be able to give detailed information regarding controls.

Mulches: Mulching, as has been reiterated again and again in answers given to questions, is an extremely valuable garden procedure. Mulches help keep moisture in the soil (I owed the survival of my tomato plants one year when I was on vacation during a drought, to a heavy mulch of grass clippings), prevent rain from splashing soil on the leaves and so help control the spread of soil-borne funguses, keep down the growth of weeds (those weeds that do grow up in the mulch are always shallow-rooted and easily removed), and, as they age and break down, add to the organic content of the soil.

Any material that is readily and inexpensively available to you can be used for a mulch. If your garden is small and exquisitely groomed, perhaps you will want to buy a mulch which will enhance its attractiveness such as buckwheat or cocoa hulls.

If you are mulching acid-loving plants, you can contribute to the well-being of the plant by using mulches which are acid in content such as shredded oak leaves, manure, pine needles, moist peat moss (I tend to shy away from this because if it ever dries out it forms a crust which sheds water), softwood sawdust and wood chips, coffee grounds, and tea leaves.

Nonacid mulches suitable for alkaline plants include: buckwheat and cocoa hulls, grass clippings, shredded leaves other than oak, salt hay, straw, hardwood sawdust, and wood chips.

For winter protection salt hay, straw, and evergreen boughs are most commonly used. Other mulches in use include: ground corn cobs, spent hops, tanbark, and bagasse. Inorganic materials may also be used for mulching: aluminum foil, glass wool, shredded newspaper, black plastic, and stones and pebbles.

All the organic mulches should be applied to a depth of about 2 inches for summer mulching, 4 to 6 inches for winter protection. In using materials such as sawdust, wood chips, and straw, remember that as they decompose they draw nitrogen from the soil depleting the amount available to the plant. Additional nitrogenous fertilizer should be used to counteract this.

2
Quick and Easy Annual Flowers

If you want to fill a garden with flowers as quickly and inexpensively as possible, plant annuals, many of which can be sown in the garden exactly where they are to bloom. Others can be started from seeds indoors in a sunny window or fluorescent-light garden, about eight to ten weeks before frost-free weather is expected where you live, or purchased as budded or just-beginning-to-bloom transplants from a local nursery or garden center.

The thing I like about annuals is that they are adapted to a wide variety of conditions and come in a rainbow of colors. In the questions and answers of this chapter I have included suggestions for the best annuals to grow in sun, shade, moist or dry soil, as ground covers, for quick screening, for fragrance, for cutting and drying, and in container gardens such as window boxes and patio planters.

If you plant annuals in well spaded and cultivated soil, in a site that receives sun or shade, depending on the needs of the individual variety, success is practically guaranteed. The difficulties usually lie in planting the seeds too deep, letting the soil dry out before the seedling roots are established, or planting a sun lover like the zinnia or rose moss in shade.

AFRICAN DAISY

Catalog descriptions make me want to try the African daisy (*Arctotis*). Is it difficult?

No, in fact I wonder that more people don't grow it, especially the blue-eyed, bluish-white *grandis*. It self-sows in my garden, but I don't think it would ever become a pest. I can depend on it for blooms over a long season every year and they are excellent for cutting. *Arctotis* needs full sun and moderately rich, well-drained soil; it is also excellent in hot, dry weather, requiring little or no irrigation if you give it a deep mulch while the soil is still moist from spring rains.

AGERATUM

Are some varieties of ageratum bluer than others, or does the color depend on the pH of the soil as it does with some forms of hydrangea?

Yes, to your first question, no to the second. Unfortunately, what is blue-blue to a catalog writer, may be lavender-blue to you. The only way to tell for sure is to purchase transplants already in bloom at your local garden center or nursery.

ANNUALS FOR A HIGH-RISE TERRACE

I have just moved into an apartment that has two small terraces, one facing south that receives full sun, the other facing east, but with no direct sun, owing to a tall building next door. This first year I'd like to fill planter boxes and hanging baskets with annual flowers. Which kinds would you recommend for the two exposures?

13

For sun I would choose fairly low-growing varieties of petunia, marigold, zinnia, ageratum, geranium, flowering tobacco, and flowering sage; to trail from hanging baskets in
sun, try sweet alyssum, rose moss, cascade-type petunias
and trailing forms of nasturtium, periwinkle, or annual
vinca, summer phlox, and verbena.

For your shaded terrace, try impatiens, coleus, lobelia,
browallia and torenia, either in pots, planters, or hanging
containers.

ANNUALS FOR CUT FLOWERS

**I enjoy having flowers outdoors in the garden as well as cut
for bouquets in the house. The trouble with me is that I
never seem to have enough for cutting without leaving the
garden looking stripped. Is there a better way?**

Yes, I suggest you grow some rows of flowers for cutting
in the vegetable garden, or in some sunny, well-drained
part of the yard where keeping all the blooms cut won't
distract from the view. My favorites for cutting include
annual or China-aster, baby's-breath, bachelor's-button,
bells-of-Ireland, cockscomb, cosmos, dianthus, larkspur,
marigold, nasturtium, flowering tobacco, petunia, snapdragon, sweet pea, and zinnia.

Since it is the nature of annuals to grow from seed to
bloom and back to mature seeds all within a single season,
it pays to keep spent blooms cut or picked before the seeds
begin to develop. This concentrates the plant's energy
always on producing more blooms instead of going to seed.

ANNUALS FOR DAMP SOIL

**The only sunny spot in my yard has soil that is poorly
drained and tends to remain damp even during long
periods of drought. Are there any annuals I could plant?**

Yes, there are some that tolerate ground that tends to dampness, but if I were you, I would build a low retaining wall, using bricks, pieces of redwood about 10 inches wide, or railroad ties, and then fill this raised planting bed with a mixture of about two parts topsoil to one each of builders' sand and sphagnum peat moss.

The annuals I have found to be the most tolerant of damp soil include browallia, pot-marigold (*Calendula*), datura, candytuft, balsam, forget-me-not (*Myosotis*), flowering tobacco, mignonette, castor-bean, torenia, vinca, and tufted pansy (*Viola cornuta*).

ANNUALS FOR DRYING

I have tried drying all kinds of flowers in silica gel in order to make winter bouquets, but frankly, it's a lot of trouble. Is there an easy way?

Yes, plant only the kinds that can be dried without special treatment. You'll find them listed as "everlastings" in the seed catalogs. Kinds like cockscomb first color the garden with fresh flowers. Then you cut them while they are still in peak condition, tie the stems in loose bunches, and hang upside down to dry in an airy, shaded place. You can make beautiful arrangements of these to enjoy indoors all fall and winter. The vivid coloring of fresh cockscomb dries to the subtle and royal shades of a fine old oriental rug. Other annuals that dry well include strawflower, statice, globe amaranth, acroclinium or helipterum, pearl everlasting, immortelle, ammobium, and rhodanthe. They combine perfectly with dried ornamental grasses such as avena, coix, and laguras.

ANNUALS FOR FRAGRANCE

My mother loves sweet-scented flowers, and since she is no longer able to do much yard work herself, I'd like to plant

a little garden mostly of annuals that are fragrant. Could you suggest some?

Yes, and what a nice idea you have! My favorite annuals that have perfumed flowers include moonflower (a vine), cleome, heliotrope, candytuft, sweet pea, sweet alyssum, stock (especially the night-scented form, *Matthiola longipetala*), forget-me-not (*Myosotis alpestris*), flowering tobacco, hybrid petunias, mignonette, nasturtium, and verbena.

ANNUALS FOR GROUND COVER

We have just moved into a new house and the yard is practically without any vegetation. Are there any low-growing annual flowers I can plant as quick coverup for the bare ground?

Although you don't say so specifically, I presume when you say there is no vegetation, that the area you want covered receives full sun. I would plant sweet alyssum, rose moss, dwarf marigolds, and the trailing forms of annual phlox, verbena, and Madagascar periwinkle.

ANNUALS FOR SCREENING

Are there any annuals that grow rapidly to several feet tall that I can use to screen my neighbor's unsightly back yard from mine? A chain-link fence, which he owns, divides us. The area receives full sun most of the day.

I would say you don't have a big problem. If you're on friendly terms, ask your neighbor if he would mind if you planted some flowering vines along the fence, explaining that you'll be glad to do all the work. If he is agreeable, choose from moonflower, cup-and-saucer vine, hyacinth-bean, morning-glory, ornamental gourd, sweet pea, black-eyed Susan vine, scarlet-runner bean or canary-bird vine (a form of nasturtium).

If planting on the fence is out of the question, select from these tall- and quick-growing annuals: hollyhock, amaranthus, giant varieties of hybrid snapdragon, cleome, cosmos, sunflower, annual hibiscus, summer-cypress (*Kochia*), castor-bean, Mexican sunflower (*Tithonia*), hedge-type hybrid marigolds, or the tallest zinnias listed in the seed catalogs.

ANNUALS FOR SHADE

Could you please suggest some annuals that will flower in an area that receives only brief periods of dappled sunlight but in shade that is fairly open and bright?

Impatiens come first to mind, but here are some others I recommend: wax begonia, Chinese forget-me-not (*Cyno-*

Browallia is available in both blue- and white-flowers. It is an excellent annual for flowers in the shade outdoors in summer. (Burpee Seeds)

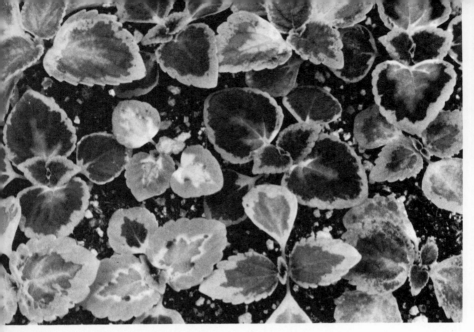

Coleus is a foliage plant with leaves of many colors. It is easy to grow from seeds; these seedlings are about four weeks old and are ready to be transplanted to individual 2- or 3-inch pots. (McDonald/Mulligan)

glossum amabile), garden balsam (*Impatiens balsamina*), lobelia, flowering tobacco (*Nicotiana alata*), mignonette, torenia, and periwinkle. Coleus would be excellent also, although it is grown for colorful foliage rather than the flowers which are not very showy.

ANNUALS FOR SUN

I live in a climate that tends to be hot and dry in the summer; in addition, the only place I have to grow flowers is in full sun. Are there any annuals I can grow?

Yes, I would say quite a number, among them abronia, amaranthus, bachelor's-button, cleome, coreopsis, cosmos, Cape-marigold (*Dimorphotheca*), California-poppy, snow-on-the-mountain (*Euphorbia marginata*), gaillardia, gazania, baby's-breath, sunflower, four-o'clock, Shirley poppy, geranium, annual phlox, rose moss (*Portulaca*), Gloriosa daisy, creeping zinnia, marigold, nasturtium, and zinnia. While all of these tolerate a certain amount of dryness in the soil, you can save on supplementary watering needs by applying a mulch all around and between the rows of these annuals as soon as they are a few inches tall in the early part of the season.

ANNUALS THAT SELF-SOW

We have recently purchased a weekend house in the country. There is a sunny meadow area where I would like to scatter seeds that would fend for themselves and come back year after year. Are there any annuals you would suggest?

Yes, Iceland and California poppies would be excellent, as well as annual dianthus, clarkia, cleome, gilia, annual baby's-breath, and larkspur. The best time to sow these seeds would be in late winter or earliest spring, ideally when there is some snow cover. Simply broadcast the seeds over the area; if there is snow, it will carry the seeds into the surface soil as it melts and they will sprout in the first warm weather. If you want them to self-sow in successive years, allow the plants to form seeds before the meadow is mown. The George W. Park Seed Company, Inc., Greenwood, S.C. 29647, offers a special mixture of annual flower seeds for growing as you have described—or you can purchase separate packets of the varieties that most appeal.

BORAGE

I know that borage is considered an herb, but its starry lavender-and-blue flowers are so pretty, couldn't I grow it along with other annuals in containers on my sunny terrace?

Yes, it is one of my favorites. In fact, I bought a started flat of borage at my local nursery several springs ago and transplanted the seedlings to a sunny spot in my flower border. In early August I cut back the longest stems almost to the ground and the new basal growth that followed gave bloom until frost. The surprise for me was that the following spring I found numerous self-sown borage seedlings in the same soil and the borage has continued to perpetuate itself year after year. All I do is thin the seedlings and cut back the old plants in August, as I described.

CABBAGE, FLOWERING

Last fall, my florist had some extraordinary potted cabbage plants, the leaves of which were crinkled, ruffled, curled, and colored in various shades of green, pink, lavender, and nearly white. Is this something I can grow in my garden?

Yes, both ornamental or flowering cabbage and kale may be cultivated outdoors the same as the edible varieties; these ornamentals are in fact edible. The best season for growing these is to sow the seeds in early summer in order for them to reach maturity in early fall while the average temperatures are going down; chilling to near freezing brings out the most beautiful coloration. Pot up the prettiest ones to enjoy indoors; prolong their life by keeping the soil moist, giving them a place in bright light, and protecting them from drafts of hot air. Once they begin to look past their prime, discard; the same plants cannot be grown again.

CHINA ASTER

Is it difficult to grow the annual China aster?

Yes, unless certain needs are met, but then, hardly any annual equals the China aster (*Callistephus chinensis*) for beauty in cut flowers. If you buy these as started plants, accept only those seedlings with healthy, crisp, green foliage. Reject any with yellow or wilted lower leaves. Whether you grow China asters from started plants or from seeds in your own garden, plant them in deeply spaded, well-drained soil. Then mulch with bark chips or cocoa bean hulls and be sure they never wilt for lack of moisture. Given this care and at least four hours direct sun daily, every plant will turn into a bouquet of bloom from midsummer to early fall.

Cosmos like this hybrid called "Goldcrest" bloom all summer in the garden, especially if you keep spent flowers picked before seeds form. (Bodger Seeds, Ltd.)

DUSTY MILLER

Is dusty miller an annual or a perennial?

Technically, all of the plants I know that are called dusty miller are perennials, but some of them, in particular the "Diamond," "Silver Queen," and "Frosty" varieties (*Senecio*, sometimes called *Cineraria*), tend to winter kill in cold climates, which makes them tender perennials. These types are easily started from seeds sown indoors in a sunny window or fluorescent-light garden in late winter. They may be transplanted outdoors as soon as there is no danger of a hard freeze.

FAREWELL-TO-SPRING

I have fallen in love with the catalog descriptions of farewell-to-spring (*Clarkia* [*Godetia*] *ahioena*). Unfortunately, I can't get it to grow well for me. What care does it need?

You have asked about an annual flower that at its best can rival a florist's azalea covered with bloom, but reaching this state is no easy matter unless you live in a climate that is both cool and dry; farewell-to-spring cannot tolerate rich, wet soil, shade, hot days or muggy nights. Otherwise, it's easy to grow. Someday when I get my greenhouse, I'm going to grow some by starting the seeds in late fall and bringing them along in the required environment of sunny coolness.

FLOWERS AT NIGHT

Are there any annual flowers that are especially effective at night? I am looking for the best kinds to plant around our outdoor living area.

Yes, I would suggest moonflower vine, evening or night-scented stock (*Matthiola longipetala*), four-o'clock, flowering tobacco, evening-primrose (*Oenothera biennis*) and any large-flowered white or pale yellow petunia. Excepting the petunia, all of these are kinds whose flowers open late in the afternoon and remain fully open through the cool evening hours, often not closing until the sun becomes hot the next morning. In addition, all of them are fragrant at night.

Hybrid geraniums like this one may be grown from seed to bloom in about three months. Give the seedlings sun or a place a few inches directly beneath the tubes in a fluorescent-light garden. (McDonald/Mulligan)

23

One of the easiest ways to have a flower garden is to fill a shallow wood planter box like this one with geraniums as soon as the weather is warm and frost-free in the spring. Full sun and low-nitrogen fertilizer bring on the blooms. (McDonald/Mulligan)

GERANIUM

I have always thought of geraniums as ready-made flowering plants that I could pick up in a sort of annual ritual some nice day in May every year at my local nursery. Now I have been reading about some outstanding hybrids that grow from seeds the same as other annual flowers. Is this true?

Yes, but if you want bloom fairly early in the season, it will be necessary to start the seeds indoors in a sunny exposure or about 3 inches below the tubes in a fluorescent-light garden. Allow at least three months from seed to bloom. And they are as easy to grow as most annual flowers that you would normally start indoors or outdoors in a protected frame—petunias and snapdragons, for example. By the way, my favorite bedding geraniums are some of the rarer varieties, some old, some new, listed by mail-order specialists such as Logee's, Merry Gardens, Carobil Farms, and Cook's Geranium Nursery (see list of by-mail sources for addresses). There are hundreds of varieties in exquisite pastels and vivid colors, both single and double flowers, that are almost never available from the usual commercial sources.

HOLLYHOCK

The hollyhocks I remember as a child always just seemed to come up; I can't recall ever seeing anyone plant them. Now I see hollyhocks listed as annuals in the seed catalogs. Are they?

Some are, some aren't; all tend toward being short-lived perennials but, since they self-sow, they also tend to behave as perennials even though some of the plants die annually. However, if you buy seeds of one of the newer hybrid forms, their self-sown offspring may not flower true to form.

25

Large, old, shrublike geraniums bring flowers and scented leaves to this combination terrace and outdoor living room. (McDonald/Mulligan)

"Fancifrills" is a recently introduced impatiens with double flowers. Grow it in the ground or in containers outdoors in warm weather. (Goldsmith Seeds)

IMPATIENS

I notice that some of the seed catalogs seem to have a far greater selection of hybrid impatiens than I can find at my local nurseries. Is this plant difficult to grow from seeds?

No, and for the same reason you have expressed, I buy my impatiens seeds from the catalogs in order to get just the right colors in plants with the size and growth habits I need for bedding in the ground in shade, for pots, window boxes, and hanging baskets, all of them in areas that are mostly shaded, except for an hour or two in the early morning and late afternoon.

27

"Cyclone" hybrid impatiens have green leaves often spectacularly variegated with white, cream, pink or salmon color; the flowers come in many colors. (McDonald/Mulligan)

Hardly any annual flower equals the impatiens for color outdoors in the shade. This hybrid is "Shady Lady." (George W. Park Seed Co., Inc.)

*Impatiens seeds sprout readily when scattered over the surface of moist,
milled sphagnum moss or vermiculite. (McDonald/Mulligan)*

I start the seeds in late February or early March by sowing
them on the surface of a sterile planting medium such as
milled or screen sphagnum moss or horticultural vermiculite. They are so small, I don't cover them at all. After
sowing, I set the pot to soak in a basin of water; when
beads of moisture show on the surface, I remove and allow
it to drain, then I enclose the entire planting, pot and all, in
a plastic bag. I place this in my fluorescent-light garden
where temperatures are around 70° F. When I can see signs
of the seedlings emerging, I begin to remove the plastic
bag, at first for an hour or two a day, gradually increasing
the time until it is no longer needed. Meanwhile, it is vital
that the growing medium be kept evenly moist, never bone
dry, and that the seedlings receive fresh, moist air that cir-
culates freely, otherwise they'll attract red spider mites.

As soon as the seedlings are large enough to handle, and
have one or two true leaves, I transplant them to individual
2- or 3-inch pots filled with a mixture of two parts all-
purpose potting soil to one each of sphagnum peat moss

When the impatiens seedlings are large enough to handle, transplant to individual 2- or 3-inch pots. Here the seedlings have been placed to grow about 10 inches below the tubes in a fluorescent-light garden. (McDonald/Mulligan)

About four-to-six weeks later the impatiens seedlings are ready to transplant outdoors. (McDonald/Mulligan)

and vermiculite. In a fluorescent-light garden, or in a window with a little direct sun, I sometimes get first blooms when the seedlings are less than three months old, or usually by the time I can set them outdoors without worry of their being frosted.

JOSEPH'S-COAT

Lately I have noticed a tall plant in gardens around here, with dark red lower leaves and a vivid pink flower or head of leaves at the top. What is this?

You have described one of the varieties of *Amaranthus tricolor*, which is sometimes called Joseph's-coat (specifically the varieties with yellow, orange, red, and pink variegation in the top leaves) and summer poinsettia. These grow from a small black seed that sprouts quickly and grows like a weed when it is sown on the surface of moist, warm soil, and lightly covered or merely firmed in place with your palm. For best results, give this plant a sunny spot and fairly moist but not rich soil. The true flowers are insignificant, but the uppermost leaves can be spectacular over a long season.

LARKSPUR

I planted larkspur seeds in my garden early last summer. Only three seedlings grew and the flowers were small and appeared only briefly; then the leaves turned yellow and the plants died. What went wrong?

First, larkspur is an annual that does best in cooler weather. For this reason, the seeds need to be planted in earliest spring when the soil first becomes workable. It is best to sow them where they are to bloom as larkspur is difficult to transplant. After the main spike of flowers begins to wither, cut back to the uppermost healthy leaves. Unless the weather is extremely hot, there should be a secondary round of bloom before heat kills the plants.

MARIGOLD

Last year I visited a beautiful garden in Ireland where I saw window boxes filled with a plant that looked like a marigold, but the leaves were finely cut like a delicate fern and the little yellow flowers were single and literally smothered the plants. It was labeled *Tagetes*. Is this available in the United States?

Yes. *Tagetes* is the Latin name for marigold. The variety you saw was probably "Golden Gem" or "Lemon Gem," both of which are listed as Signet marigolds in the catalog of the

W. Atlee Burpee Company, Warminster, Pa. 18974. Besides window boxes, I find these are excellent for planting in hanging baskets that receive a half day or more of direct sun.

I thought marigolds were foolproof, but all of mine developed yellow-flecked leaves last summer, with tiny spider-like webs all over. What was wrong?

Red spider mites. You're right, marigolds hardly ever fail, but if the soil in which they are growing is allowed to dry out severely, frequently red spider mites may attack. Avoid by keeping the soil evenly moist; if mites appear despite this good care, hose the leaves down twice a day with water. If the mites persist, spray with a miticide such as Kelthane, following label directions as to amount and frequency.

Marigolds like this "First Lady" hybrid will bloom from early summer to frost if the spent blooms are kept picked off. For success in growing as container plants, be sure to keep the soil moist; provide at least a half day of direct sunlight. (Burpee Seeds)

Marigold seeds are among the easiest to sprout. These have been started in 2-inch peat pots filled with vermiculite; now they are ready for transplanting outdoors. (United States Department of Agriculture)

Nasturtiums make spectacular hanging plants. Start the seeds in the soil where they are to grow; provide sun and enough water to prevent severe dryness at any time. (McDonald/Mulligan)

NASTURTIUM

What could cause my nasturtiums to go almost entirely to leaves and produce only a few flowers?

Soil that is too rich in nitrogen content or a site that does not receive at least a half day of direct sunlight. Nasturtiums, like rose moss (*Portulaca*), do best in sandy, lean soil.

Nasturtiums are one of my favorite flowers, but some kind of bug always eats them up just about the time they are beginning to bloom. Is there an easy solution?

Yes, if you don't mind spraying your nasturtiums with an all-purpose flower-garden pesticide at the first sign of the bugs, which are probably a form of aphids. However, if you are planning to eat some of the flowers in a tossed salad (and they are delicious), be sure to use an insecticide labeled as being safe to use on food crops.

PETUNIA

My petunias do well every year until around the middle of August. Then they begin to sprawl and go all to seed. Am I neglecting some special care?

Yes, after several weeks of heavy bloom, cut back the longest stems to an inch or two from the ground. Apply a light side dressing of granular fertilizer around the plants, lightly scratch into the surface soil, then water well. This treatment will encourage compact new growth from the base and prolong the flowering season until frost.

Last year I purchased flats of petunias in bloom at my garden center and set them into my garden. They were beautiful all summer, right up until frost. This spring when I began to clear the ground, I found numerous petunia seed-

lings already well along. So I thinned and transplanted them. They grew well but the flowers were not anything like those from last year; the colors were dull and the size didn't begin to measure up. Is this because I didn't fertilize them properly?

No. Petunias have highly mixed parentage. Your self-sown seedlings have reverted back to earlier, less desirable forms. The only way to avoid this happening again is always to start fresh each year with hybrid seeds, which you can start indoors in a sunny window or fluorescent-light garden about two months ahead of frost-free weather outdoors, or with transplants from your local garden center or nursery.

White or pale yellow hybrid petunias like "Summer Sun" are excellent for planting near an outdoor living area since the flowers show up well by moonlight; they are also scented in the evening. (McDonald/Mulligan)

Petunias will flower in either full sun or part shade, as in this raised planting bed. Cut back long, straggly growth in midsummer to promote strong basal shoots for later bloom. (Maynard Parker)

"Ruby Magic" hybrid petunia has flowers in a dark, velvety burgundy color. The easiest way to have petunias is to purchase started seedlings in flats like this one; purchasing after the flowers are open allows selection of exactly the color you have in mind. (McDonald/Mulligan)

Iceland poppies are hardy annuals. Sow the seeds outdoors over well-prepared soil (or snow) in winter or early spring. (James McNair)

Verbena is one of the best annuals for use as a ground cover or hanging basket plant in full sun. (McDonald/Mulligan)

ROSE MOSS

Rose moss grows like a weed in my neighbor's yard, but I can't succeed with it. Is there some secret I should know about?

Well, I wouldn't call it a secret, but rose moss (*Portulaca*) needs full sun and sandy, well-drained soil that is not too rich. If you have a piece of ground that is bare, hot, and dry in the summer, this plant is superb. Broadcast the seeds where they are to grow. More will sprout if you moisten the area by misting with water after sowing, and then lightly mulch with a scant layer of straw. The newest and best kinds of rose moss are F_1 hybrids, a designation you'll find on seed packets of the best varieties of all annuals.

SNAPDRAGON

Are there any hybrid snapdragons that will do well in my climate where the summers tend to be very hot?

Yes, I recommend the "Rocket" series of hybrids, which are readily obtainable from most major seed companies, either by separate color (George W. Park Seed Co., Inc., Greenwood, S.C. 29647, lists twelve different colors) or in a mix-

For best results, snapdragons need well-cultivated soil in a place that receives direct sun for at least four or five hours daily. Keep spent flowers cut in order to promote more bloom. (Maynard Parker)

The flowers of Liberty Bell snapdragon are open trumpets rather than the usual form. (Burpee Seeds)

ture. With regard to the "Rocket" hybrids, Park advises, "These were purposely bred for garden use and hot weather tolerance. They grow 30 to 36 inches tall, producing long spikes with many closely spaced florets; ideal for garden decorating or for use as cut flowers. Rockets bloom magnificently in midsummer. Cut spikes back to top of leaves and they will bloom even more in the fall."

Annual vinca, or periwinkle, is available in dwarf, trailing varieties like this one, for use as a ground cover, in hanging containers, or in more upright forms. (George W. Park Seed Co., Inc.)

Wax begonia seeds are tiny. Scatter them over the surface of milled (screened) sphagnum moss; keep constantly moist and warm in bright light or in a fluorescent-light garden. Allow at least three months from seed to first bloom. (McDonald/Mulligan)

SWEET ALYSSUM

Sweet alyssum is one of my favorite annuals, but how can I keep it from going all to seed and dying out early in the season?

Shear back all the flowering stems after each period of heavy bloom. Where I live, seeds started indoors in March or April and placed outside toward the end of May usually bloom heavily in June, then I shear off the spent flower heads and another crop appears in a couple of weeks. I repeat the procedure until cold weather takes over.

WAX BEGONIA

Is it natural for some wax begonias (*B. semperfloreus*) to have all-green leaves and others to be reddish bronze?

Yes, although some direct sun is needed in order to bring out the richest coloring in the bronze-leaf varieties.

Last year I purchased started plants of wax begonias and set them outdoors for the summer in my garden. They were compact-growing and covered with flowers until just before frost, at which time I cut them back and brought them indoors to a sunny plant room for the winter. Now the weather is warm enough to put them back outdoors for this summer, but they are all tall and spindly looking. What should I do?

Ideally, pitch the old begonias and start fresh with hybrid seedlings just beginning to flower from your local garden center or nursery. Semperflorens begonias really do best in the first season they flower from seeds. However, if you can't afford to start over every year, here is the procedure I have followed, with fairly satisfactory results: Cut back all the old stems to about 2 inches, but leave any new growth appearing at the base. Set the plants outdoors in bright

Wax begonias perform best when started annually from hybrid seeds. (McDonald/Mulligan)

light but little or no direct sun until they become accustomed to the open air, then you can gradually increase the amount of exposure to direct sun. If you give them some fresh soil and good care in general, they should make a fairly decent showing within four to six weeks. The stems you pruned off can be used as tip cuttings, but I find that these in particular tend to make inferior plants that are too inclined to grow tall and weak with very little branching.

Please help settle a long-standing argument, friendly of course, between my neighbor and me. She says that wax begonias will not grow outdoors in full sun. I say they will. Who is right?

I tend to agree with you, but wax begonias growing in full sun need to be watered often enough to keep the soil moist at all times. Otherwise, the leaves will burn badly in full sun if the roots are thirsty for water.

ZINNIA

My zinnias grow beautifully every year until about August, then the leaves develop a kind of white mold. Can this be prevented?

You have described powdery mildew, a disease that favors, besides zinnias, roses, lilacs, and summer phlox. It will help to plant your zinnias with extra wide spacing to allow freer air circulation, but in climates where late summer usually brings warm, sunny days, followed by a sharp drop in temperatures at night, powdery mildew is almost inevitable unless you maintain a regular spraying or dusting program using a fungicide such as Maneb or Captan.

Creeping zinnia, or sanvitalia, covers its trailing stems with golden-yellow flowers all summer. Give it full sun. (McDonald/Mulligan)

3

Biennials: Spectacular Flowers the Second Season

Biennials are plants which are sown one year, make vegetative growth, then flower the following year, after which their life span is over. Fortunately, except under the most harsh climatic conditions, many of them self-sow and so propagate themselves. With luck they may seem to be perennial plants, requiring only that the seedlings be thinned to permit the remaining ones adequate growing room.

Actually because most biennials are easily transplanted, one common way of using them in the flower border is to start the seedlings off in an out of the way spot and move them at the beginning of their second year, just before they are ready to bloom, creating a spot of instant color in the flower bed. After blooming, particularly if self-sown seedlings are not wanted, the biennial can be consigned to the compost heap to be replaced with a later-flowering annual. However, if the flowers are kept picked so they do not go to seed, some biennials will bloom for a long season and see the summer through.

Despite their brief life span, biennials are valuable for they include some of the more colorful and beautifully scented of garden varieties and their imaginative use can do much to enhance the blooming garden.

CANTERBURY BELLS

I bought some Canterbury bells of the cup-and-saucer kind but they did not flower very well. This year they did not come up at all. How can I get these flowers to bloom and winter over in southern Wisconsin?

Canterbury bells are a biennial (*Campanula medium*) which will winter over in the North with the protection of a mulch except where winters are most severe. In those areas, Canterbury bells should be dug and wintered in a cold frame. For best flowering performance they need partial shade and a good, slightly alkaline garden soil that drains perfectly. You will get a longer period of bloom if you keep the flowers cut as they wither.

In the garden, Canterbury bells combine well with other June-blooming biennials and perennials such as columbine, achillea, evening-primrose, and lily. (McDonald/Mulligan)

Cup-and-saucer Canterbury bells are among the most treasured of the biennial flowers. They are available in white, blue, and pink varieties. (George W. Park Seed Co., Inc.)

ENGLISH DAISY

I edged a border with English daisies but as summer went on they shriveled up and turned brown. Will they come back next year? I live in Kansas.

English daisy (*Bellis perennis*) is a perennial treated as a biennial under most growing conditions in this country. Planted in the cool summers of coastal areas where winters are not too severe, they thrive and bloom all summer and self-sow freely for a return appearance the next spring. They do not take to hot dry summers, such as you have, and you must think of them as a charming spring annual or go to some extra trouble to keep them going.

You might try digging them up after the flowers have bloomed, separate the clumps into smaller ones, and replant them in a cooler spot where they don't get full sun. Keep the soil moist. In the fall, lift them again and replant them where they were originally flowering for more bloom next spring. Mulch them with loose material such as salt hay. If your winters are very severe, it would be better to winter them in a cold frame.

FOXGLOVE

I was told foxgloves were biennials, but I have several in my perennial border and they come back year after year. Can you explain this?

Some species of foxglove (*Digitalis*) are perennial, while some of the biennial ones reseed themselves quite reliably if the soil is not dug up, so that in effect they too function as perennials.

Foxgloves can be made to bloom for a longer season by cutting off the main spike when the blossoms fade, encouraging the development of side shoots.

HONESTY

Is honesty difficult to grow? I would like to raise some to have the circular flowers for dried arrangements.

Honesty, or money plant as it is called in some parts of the country (*Lunaria annua*), is not at all difficult to grow. It adapts to most garden conditions, including some shade, and has no special soil requirements. As a matter of fact, although it is considered a biennial, it self-sows so freely that it is sometimes considered a pest. The seed pods are the papery circles that are used for dried arrangements. The actual flowers most often are purple, although there are white and crimson varieties as well. It is easily raised from seed and should be started in an out of the way place. As with all biennials, it blooms the second year. In the fall the plants are moved to where you want to grow them.

PANSY

I bought and planted last year a flat of large-flowered pansies. They flowered moderately well, though they did not produce well toward the end of the season. This summer there are many plants with little flowers, instead of the large ones I purchased. Can you explain this?

Pansies (*Viola tricolor hortensis*) are a short-lived perennial, treated as a biennial or an annual, particularly in mild-winter sections of the country. I suspect from what you say that you did not keep the pansies picked, so that they have reseeded themselves and some seedlings have reverted to the original wild plant, the Johnny-jump-up.

Pansies should be planted in rich soil which is kept moist and where there will be shade from midday sun. They will bloom freely for a long season if the flowers are picked weekly. (They make charming little nosegays indoors.) Otherwise old flowers will set seed and all their energy will turn to seed production, resulting in fewer or no new flowers. The self-sown seeds very often lose their hybrid qualities. When the plants grow leggy, cut them back almost to the ground to induce new growth and flowering. At this time it would be wise to give them a liquid feeding.

They are easily raised both from side cuttings and from seed. But buy hybrid seed rather than trying to save your own. Seed should be sown in the fall, the little plants wintered over in a cold frame and planted out in the spring. Cuttings grow easily from young side shoots planted in a mixture of equal parts of soil and sand in a cold frame. In warm climates, seed and cuttings can be started in the open.

EVENING-PRIMROSE

My biennial evening-primroses self-seeded to such a degree that there were many large plants crowding each other out. This year I transplanted them a suitable distance apart but they did not survive. What happened?

Evening-primrose (*Oenothera biennis*) should be transplanted only when the seedlings are small as the roots are easily damaged when the plants are larger.

SWEET WILLIAM

My sweet William is blooming beautifully this year but I have been told it will not come up next year. Is this so?

Although actually a perennial, sweet William (*Dianthus barbatus*) is most commonly treated as a biennial. It has been my experience that, except in extreme cold areas of the country, it can be kept for a number of years with proper care. Sweet William does well in ordinary garden soil, or a somewhat sandy one where drainage is good. Division every two years keep them coming along.

51

4

All-Season Bloom from Carefree Perennials

Perennials are the mainstay of the flowering garden. These are the plants that come back year after year (although some are longer-lived than others) if some minimal care and attention is given them. Some are more carefree than others.

Few gardens today provide the space for the classical perennial border so popular for generations in England. If you have room and a desire for a large perennial border, this certainly is one of the most impressive of garden displays. At the same time no garden is really complete without a few choice perennials. Lacking the room for lavish planting, small, less formal beds can be planned to take advantage of these reliable plants. Or an occasional clump can be planted between or in front of shrubs and small trees. Most perennials make a better showing if a group of at least three are planted together.

With judicious planning, a garden can boast of colorful blooms for as long as the weather permits where you live. There are perennials which bloom early in the season, in midsummer and on into the fall. A number of perennials can be induced to bloom a second time by cutting off the spent flower heads after their first bloom. These are dealt with in the answers to specific questions.

Plant your garden with the flowering period of each plant

in mind. Study garden catalogs and the stock at local garden centers to find those which suit your taste, growing conditions, and space. Besides the ultimate size of the plant, in planning to use perennials, keep in mind not only the season of bloom and the color of the flowers, but the texture and color of the foliage and whether the latter remains in evidence all season, or whether the plant disappears after blooming as do, for instance, columbine.

As well as the above considerations, group plants for similarity of growing needs. You will complicate your gardening enormously if alkaline-loving perennials needing loose, fast-draining soil, such as bluebells, are planted next to moisture- and acid-loving ones such as lady's-slippers. In the long run, neither one will do well. If your soil is naturally alkaline and the space you have for growing perennials is in full sun, it is wisest to choose plants that do well under those conditions. Similarly, for an acid soil in partial shade, choose plants that need those circumstances to thrive.

In time most perennials will form such dense clumps that they will need to be "lifted" (dug up from the flower bed with the soil intact around their roots) and divided. The technique of dividing can be accomplished by pulling them apart by hand into smaller sections if they are small plants; larger ones can be forced apart by plunging two spading forks, back-to-back, in the center of the plant mass and maneuvering the forks so the division is accomplished, or simply by cutting them apart with shears. Very often the dense center which was the original plant will have died and can be cut off and discarded. The stronger healthy outside portions can then be replanted to increase the number of plants in the garden, or can be shared with friends.

ASTER, PERENNIAL

My perennial asters have developed a disease. Some of the stems are brown and black and the leaves on these stems are turning yellow and dying. Is there anything I can do to save them?

The symptoms you describe are those of a fungus disease called wilt. It is most likely to develop in cool, wet, spring weather and is in the root system. It affects many plants, and plant breeders are constantly working to develop new varieties which are resistant. The only control is to lift and destroy these roots and replant only flowers that are not subject to wilt where the asters grew before.

You can save the asters you have (also known as Michaelmas daisy) by growing new plants from cuttings. Take only strong, healthy cuttings in the spring. Make a clean cut ¼ to ½ inch below the lowest set of leaves. Remove the lowest set of leaves, dust the base of the cutting with rooting hormone, and insert into a rooting medium. Vermiculite, a mixture of sand and peat, a mixture of vermiculite and perlite or the commercially prepared soilless

Butterfly milk weed, Asclepias tuberosa, *opens orange flowers in late summer. It is a wild flower that also makes an outstanding garden perennial in sunlight and well-drained soil. (McDonald/Mulligan)*

mixes are all good rooting mediums. If you have a green-house, a hotbed or a propagating case, set the cuttings in individual small pots. They will need to be kept well wa-tered and in a humid atmosphere until they are rooted and can be planted in the garden. Otherwise, use a bulb or azalea pot (both wider and not as deep as ordinary pots). In the center of the rooting medium in this pot, bury to its rim a 2-inch clay pot in which the drainage hole has been stopped up. (The hole can be sealed with a small cork and paraffin or a bit of clay.) Fill the small pot with water and in-sert the cuttings around it. Put the pot with the cuttings in a large plastic bag and place it in bright light, but not in direct sunlight. Keep the center pot filled with water. This will keep the cuttings evenly moist. You can check the root development by lifting the inner pot. The roots will show as they grow through the rooting medium.

When they are well rooted, plant in a new place in the flower bed where no plants with wilt grew before. They should bloom the first year.

ASTILBE

It is always difficult to find things that tolerate salt air at my seashore garden. I was delighted to find an astilbe plant seemed to thrive, and I planted more of them. I dug soil-building material and fertilizer into the sandy soil at plant-ing time, but after a few years they are not doing well. Do they just grow old and need to be discarded?

No, astilbe (meadowsweet) can be kept going, but they do have to be lifted and divided every three years. They are what are known as "gross feeders," that is they need a good deal of fertilizer and rich soil that will retain moisture. Your astilbe needs to be dug, the soil reworked (they are shallow-rooted so it need not be deeply dug), and more organic ma-terial such as compost, rotted manure, and peat moss, as well as fertilizer, worked in. Then divide and replant the clumps; early spring is the best time to do this.

BABY'S-BREATH

My perennial baby's-breath "Bristol Fairy" was disappointing last year although I saw others blooming in neighboring gardens long after mine had gone by.

The perennial baby's-breath (*Gypsophila paniculata*) of which the double-flowered "Bristol Fairy" is currently a favored variety, will perform best in full sun in soil enriched with manure or compost. If the soil is acid, ground limestone should be used. "Bristol Fairy" is grafted on the roots of the single-flowered parent species and the graft should be set at least an inch below the soil. It will bloom for a longer period if seeds are not allowed to form. Cut the spent flowers off and it will bloom again. At its best it may grow to be a large sprawling plant 4 feet wide and may need staking.

BELLFLOWER, PEACH-LEAVED

I cannot seem to be successful with peach-leaved bellflowers. They simply do not thrive and flower. What can be the cause of failure?

The peach-leaved bellflower, also called peach-leafed bluebell, harebell, or peach bells (*Campanula percisifolia*), is generally a trouble-free plant providing it is in average good garden soil. It tolerates sun or partial shade. It occurs to me perhaps your soil is too acid. Test your soil and, if the pH is below 6.0, lift your plants and dig some lime into the bed, then replant. Bellflowers will also bloom for a longer period if the dead flowers are kept picked off.

Baby's-breath, available in both annual and perennial types, with flowers that are double (as shown at right) or single, is excellent for garden bloom, but is treasured mostly as a cut flower, to be used either fresh or air-dried. (McDonald/Mulligan)

BELLFLOWER, ITALIAN

I have heard Italian bellflower recommended as a perfect plant to grow on a rock wall. Will it grow and bloom in Monterey, California?

Italian bellflower (*Campanula isophylla*), also called star of Bethlehem, should grow ideally in your mild-winter coastal climate and be most effective cascading over a rock wall. It requires a well-drained gritty soil with added humus. It should be in filtered sunlight. Fertilize it with a high-phosphorus plant food (5-10-5) in spring and summer and make sure it is watered frequently. During the winter it can go almost dry. You can also grow it effectively as a hanging basket plant.

BLEEDING-HEART

My bleeding-heart bloomed nicely last spring, but then summer came, and now (late winter) it seems to have disappeared. Did it die?

After blooming in the spring, bleeding-heart (*Dicentra spectabilis*) does lose its foilage if planted in full sun. It does somewhat better planted in rich, moist soil in partial shade. It does not move successfully so it is best to leave it where it is growing and fill in around it with annuals or spreading perennials that fill out later in the season. In the spring you will find the plant did not die, just to the ground.

In the Northeast, dicentra is a long-lived perennial. In hot southern areas it is customary to treat it more as an annual, replacing when the foliage disappears and fails to return.

Fringed bleeding-heart, although it has smaller blooms of lighter pink, keeps its blue-gray foilage so might be a better choice for a sunny location. It also has a longer blooming season—from May to August. Bleeding-heart is also known as Dutchman's breeches and squirrel corn.

Fernleaf bleeding-heart, Dicentra eximia, *blooms over a long season, provided it receives dappled sunlight in summer and the soil is kept moist.* (McDonald/Mulligan)

SIBERIAN BUGLOSS

I have been looking for a trouble-free perennial with blue flowers to plant in a damp, partially shaded location near a pond shaded by some tall willows.

Siberian bugloss (*Brunnera macrophylla*) is a good choice. The heart-shaped leaves eventually will form nice clumps and may be grown for years before they need division.

Hardy perennial chrysanthemums are available in many sizes and colors; also in varieties that bloom early (mid-to-late August), midseason and late (right up to Thanksgiving, or hard freezing). This one is called Yorktown. (Thon's Garden Mums)

Not all hardy perennial chrysanthemums have ordinary flowers—this one is in the more exotic spider form. (Thon's Garden Mums)

CHRYSANTHEMUM

We are in Nova Scotia and have planted winter-hardy chrysanthemums. However, our summer is so short that frequently the first frost occurs just after the blossoms have opened so we do not get to enjoy them. Is there anything to be done to prevent this?

As you probably know, chrysanthemums are short-day plants, which is to say they only set their bloom as the days grow short. You might try transplanting them to a different place in your garden to where they do get some midday sun, which they need to bloom, but where they are shaded either early in the morning or late in the afternoon thus artificially shortening their day prematurely. This may give them a short enough day to bloom earlier. The other solution is to plant earlier-blooming varieties.

My chrysanthemums look healthy enough but they grow tall and leggy with not too many flowers. Should I replace them with cushion mums?

Two things come to mind immediately when you say your chrysanthemums become leggy and flower poorly. First, do you divide the clumps in the spring? When the new growth is 6 to 12 inches tall, dig the old plant, remove the sturdy outer shoots, dividing them so there are one to three shoots in each clump. Don't replant the old center. Although this is troublesome, you get a dividend in the form of many new plants. Chrysanthemums are heavy feeders so they should be replanted 18 inches apart in rich garden soil which has had manure, compost or leaf mold added and supplemented with fertilizer such as phosphate rock and bone meal or a chemical fertilizer with a reading of 5-10-5. As the new plants grow, they can be fed with manure tea weekly or every two weeks with plant food.

The second thing chrysanthemums need in order to become bushy is regular pinching. As soon as the shoots are 6 inches tall, the growing tips should be pinched out. This will induce side shoots to grow out. In turn, they are pinched out to produce more side shoots. Keep on pinching the growing tips and buds off every three or four weeks. until mid-July. The plants will be bushy and spreading and covered with flowers.

If all the above is more than you have time for, then cushion mums are the answer. They are low and shrubby on their own and bloom quite freely.

COLUMBINE

A showy planting of columbines in my perennial garden has not reappeared this spring. What destroyed them?

Unfortunately, although hybridizers have produced larger flowers and longer spurs on columbines, many of the newer varieties seem to be short-lived. The older, less showy European columbine (*Aquilegia vulgaris*) is long lived but not as attractive. These graceful hybrids need not be overlooked since all varieties are easily grown from seeds. Sow some seeds every second year and move the new plants to the flower bed the following year.

Can you tell me how to make my columbines bloom more profusely?

Columbines are not very fussy about their growing conditions but, as with all plants, will grow their best in soil which has been well prepared with soil-building materials such as rotted manure, peat moss or compost. They do need good drainage but do not appreciate drying out. They will grow and flower in full sun or partial shade, but the latter seems to result in a longer period of bloom.

Plant the clumps 18 inches apart to allow space for the mature columbines. When the plants are young the bare spots can be filled in with annuals. By removing the faded flowers before the seed pods can form, you will extend the blooming period by several weeks. Or the old stems can be cut back all at once to bring on a second period of bloom.

CORAL BELLS

Some heucheras planted last fall are not growing well and are not blooming. As a matter of fact, they look half dead.

If you live in a cold winter climate, coral bells (*Heuchera sanguinea*) do better planted in the spring. Fall planted ones have not had time to have their roots take hold so alternate freezing and thawing in winters heaves the roots out of the ground. Try to save them by lifting them and removing the dead portions. Plant the healthy sections in light, loamy soil where the drainage is good. (It can be in partial shade.) Give them a good mulch this winter after the ground freezes.

(I cannot grow coral bells at all because the deer who roam our grounds find the tender evergreen leaves delectable and munch them right down to the ground.)

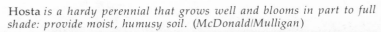

Hosta *is a hardy perennial that grows well and blooms in part to full shade: provide moist, humusy soil. (McDonald/Mulligan)*

DAISY, SHASTA

We have several clumps of both single and double Shasta daisies in our perennial border. The singles are magnificent but the doubles never do as well. Is it just that the doubles are more delicate?

I think the fact that you are growing the single and double Shasta daisies (*Chrysanthemum maximum*) together in your perennial border gives me a clue to your problem. Single Shasta daisies flourish in full sun, but the double varieties require partial shade to do their best.

Tall-bearded iris are among the most beautiful of hardy perennial flowers. Plant the rhizomes in late July or August, and in full sun and well-drained soil. Divide and replant every three or four years. (Maynard Parker)

DELPHINIUMS

What are the correct growing conditions for Pacific giant delphiniums? They seem to grow poorly for me.

You do not give your address and I cannot tell where you live. These hybrid delphiniums are hardy, but not long-lived plants. They do not thrive in areas of intense summer heat and mild winters. In the south most species are treated as annuals. The ideal planting site for them is in full sun, with good air circulation but where they are protected from wind. In shade or with poor circulation of air the stalks will be leggy with scant bloom.

The bed in which these tall hybrids are planted should be deeply dug. Since manure seems to encourage crown rot, it should only be used in the deeper part of the soil. Compost and bone meal should be worked into the soil and, if it is heavy soil, mix in sand as well.

The pH of the soil should be neutral or slightly alkaline. If the pH is lower than 6.0, ground limestone should also be added. Space the plants 2 feet apart. A scattering of wood ashes around them will also help maintain the alkalinity of the soil and discourage slugs which are especially fond of delphinium foilage. During dry seasons the ground around them should be soaked at least once a week. Avoid getting water on the leaves as delphiniums are prone to fungal diseases.

When the flowering stalks appear, some of the weaker ones may be cut out to encourage larger blossoms on the remaining ones. Staking will be needed to support the heavy spikes. After the first bloom, cut the stalks back to large leaves to encourage a second crop of blossoms. In the fall cut the stalks down to the ground so the hollow stems do not fill with rainwater and induce crown rot. Mulch as recommended in the answer to the following question.

I mulched my Pacific hybrid delphiniums with leaves this winter to prevent heaving and they developed crown rot. Should they not be mulched?

Delphiniums are so susceptible to crown rot (this means the part of the plant which is above ground, exclusive of the stems, rots away from molds present in water) that any mulch that retains moisture is likely to help it develop. The best mulch to prevent heaving in winter is a mixture of sand and crushed charcoal. (Use charcoal sold especially for horticultural purposes, not that sold for barbecuing.) Coal ashes used to be recommended but I don't imagine they are widely available these days. The same mixture can also be used around the plant during the growing season to facilitate drainage. A loose covering of salt hay would also serve.

Should one, or should one not fertilize delphiniums for better bloom? It has been my experience that they are best left to themselves, but a friend of mine maintains they need to be well fertilized before and after blooming.

This does seem to be an area of general disagreement but, at present, it is thought that the single-flowered, low-growing varieties do best in soil which is only of average fertility. Too much fertilizer tends to make the spikes grow tall and leggy without achieving any improvement in the blossoms.

On the other hand, the large-flowered types which grow several feet high, such as the Giant Pacific hybrids, profit by good feeding which should, as your friend recommends, be scratched into the soil near the crown in early spring and after the plant has bloomed. Use bone meal or a fertilizer high in phosphorus. While the plant is blooming it can also be fed a liquid plant food biweekly.

Since delphiniums are prone to crown rot and fungal diseases, avoid using manures as they seem to encourage the development of diseases. Compost mixed with phosphate rock and potash rock may be used, or chemical fertilizers with a high phosphate content such as 5-10-5 or 12-16-12.

Is it possible to grow delphiniums from seeds forming on my present plants?

Yes, delphiniums grow readily from seed. The hybrids do not all come true to color so it is best to plant them in an out of the way place. The first year the plants will not bloom much, but you will be able to judge which are superior and move them to your perennial garden, discarding the others.

Seed should be sown as soon as it is ripe in the fall. Do not fertilize the soil in which they are to be sown but add some sand for good rapid drainage. Plant the seeds no deeper than twice the narrower width of the seeds. Firm fine soil over them and cover with damp burlap or cheese cloth so that they are not washed out by rain. The following fall, transplant the choice seedlings to the garden bed for lovely bloom the following year.

If you are not able to plant the seeds in the fall, collect them in an envelope, seal the envelope in a small airtight jar, and keep the jar in the refrigerator till spring planting time.

"Bee-balm," or monarda, is a hardy perennial with mauve, purple, or brilliant red flowers that put on their most spectacular show in August and early September. (McDonald/Mulligan)

FUCHSIA

We live in northwest Washington State on Puget Sound. I would like to grow fuchsias in flower beds in my garden. I know our foggy, rainy temperature is just right for them in summer, but are there any winter-hardy ones that can be planted outdoors for summer that bloom?

Your summer climate is certainly ideal for fuchsias and, except for some of the more tender hybrids intended for greenhouse culture, there are varieties you should be able to grow in your garden. *Fuchsia magellanica* is relatively hardy; its variety "riccartonii" is especially so. It will lose its leaves with frost and die back in freezing weather. To be sure it will winter over, mound sawdust or compost to a depth of 6 inches over the plant. When the weather warms up and danger of frost is past, remove the sawdust and prune back to healthy wood.

GASPLANT

I divided my gasplants two years ago and they have not bloomed since. What happened to them?

Gasplant, or fraxinella (*Dictamnus albus*), resents transplanting and should only be divided when it becomes absolutely necessary. When the plants must be divided, you can expect them to take some time to reestablish themselves. It will be two or three years before they will bloom as they did before division.

LADY'S-SLIPPER

Some years ago I successfully rescued some yellow lady's-slippers from a building site that was being bulldozed for a shopping center and planted them in a moist shady location in my garden. They did well for several years but are now blooming sparsely. What can I do for them?

The key to success with most wildlings is to try to duplicate the conditions under which they grow in nature. Obviously you did this successfully when you transplanted them, as is evidenced by the success you had in establishing them—no mean feat! Lady's-slippers, including the yellow lady's-slipper (*Cypripedium calceolus pubescens*), are notoriously difficult to transplant. In the wild they are usually found growing among deciduous trees so that they get filtered light—not dense shade. I wonder if since you planted them the trees or shrubs that are shading them have grown so dense that too little light is getting to your lady's-slippers?

Also, in their native habitat, as the leaves fall off the trees, they have an annual top dressing of gradually decomposing leaves. You should duplicate this by an annual top dressing of leaf mold or damp peat moss.

Lady's-slipper is also known as mocassin flower.

LUPINE

Can I grow lupines north of San Francisco? If so, how?

Yes, you are in one of the sections of the country where lupines are at their best as they need cool, humid summers to put on their best showing. Where summers are hot and dry, they do not bloom and grow well. The best perennial type available are the Russell hybrids. They grow in tall dense spikes in a wide variety of colors.

You can buy container-grown plants or start your own from seed. Plant seeds when the weather is warm or start them earlier in the spring in a cold frame in individual pots. The large seeds must have their husks nicked or they must be soaked in warm water overnight in order to hasten germination. Those started in a cold frame may be moved to a bed when the weather is warm.

Lupines have far-reaching roots and do not transplant successfully after they are a year old. The seedlings should be moved where they are to grow in October or spring. For best growth they should have a sunny bed deeply dug with well-rotted manure or compost added. Space 3 feet apart.

PEONIES

Why don't my peonies bloom? They get six hours of sun a day, which I'm told is adequate. They were planted three years ago and, although they have grown full and shrubby during this time, they don't flower.

Peonies often do not bloom because they have been planted too deeply. The roots should not be planted with the eyes or buds more than 1 or 2 inches below the soil surface. Deeper planting inhibits blooming.

This fall, dig your peonies and reset them so they are planted shallowly. They probably won't bloom next spring but should in following years. Also, early each spring try sprinkling some wood ashes from a fireplace around the emerging shoots. Cultivate the ashes in lightly, being careful not to injure the shoots. If you don't have access to wood ashes, use bone meal or a good all-purpose fertilizer. Feed them again after their blooming period is over with bone meal or commercial fertilizer.

When we moved from Connecticut to southern Arizona, I brought some roots and cuttings of plant favorites from my garden. Among them were peonies. They are growing, but do not bloom well. Can you tell me what to do?

Peonies are one of the herbaceous plants that need a cold winter nap in order to bloom well. They need to have the leaves die back to the ground which they cannot do satisfactorily in the southern Arizona climate. There has been some progress in developing peonies that will tolerate more heat, and I suggest you try local nurseries near your home to see if there are varieties that will bloom in your locality.

This glorious white flower is from a hybrid tree peony, one of the flower garden's choicest plants. (Louis Smirnow)

PHLOX

Several years ago I purchased and planted some named varieties of phlox. The flowers were in blues and pinks and they made a lovely showing. This year the blooms are all a muddy magenta color. Why did this happen?

Hybrids of *Phlox paniculata* need to have the flowering heads removed after bloom. If this is not done, seed heads will form and the plants will reseed themselves. Since the hybrids do not grow true from seed, the resulting seedlings

Summer phlox, especially hybrids like this one by Symons-Jeune, give bouquets of bloom from July to September. Plant the roots in autumn or early spring. (McDonald/Mulligan)

will be of the original parent, *P. paniculata*. Eventually these new plants will take over and crowd out the less hardy fancy varieties so that you wind up with a bed of the less attractively colored old species. The older white hybrid "Miss Lingard" seems to avoid this and remains happily white.

It is worth your while to remove the old flower clusters as, in addition to avoiding reseeding, the process will also promote some later bloom.

My garden phlox, which are now three years old, have never bloomed satisfactorily. How can I encourage them to do better?

To do their best phlox do need some attention. Most important, of course, is that they should have been planted in a well-dug soil with rotted manure or other moisture-retaining material added. Their roots are near the surface and

Hardy violets, species of Viola, *make wonderful ground cover plants in shady places where the soil is usually moist. There are single- and double-flowered forms, mainly either white or purple. (McDonald/Mulligan)*

there should be a mulch to keep these roots moist. If they are planted in light soil or where summers are very hot, they should be in partial shade. In cooler areas they can have more sun. If your present growing conditions do not meet with the above, it would be wise to transplant your phlox. This is most successfully done in early spring or early fall.

In early spring, lightly cultivate bone meal or other good fertilizer into the soil around the plants. When the plants are 2 feet high, supplement this with liquid feeding. Remove weak shoots. Keep the plants well watered while they are growing, being careful to not wet the leaves since phlox are subject to mildew. Dust with sulfur or a commercial preparation to help prevent mildew. Pinching back a couple of stalks in each group will aid the formation of a few later blooms.

Keep flower clusters cut off after they fade. In the fall, cut the clumps back to about 2 inches. Divide the clumps in the fall every three to five years.

POPPY, ORIENTAL

Divisions of Oriental poppies given me by a neighbor have not bloomed. Hers have always been breathtaking. What did I do wrong?

You probably have not done anything wrong. Poppies resent being moved and usually do not bloom the first year after transplanting. August is the best time to divide them. If you have good healthy foliage growth, they will probably bloom next year.

They should be planted where there is at least a half day of sun, in a well-drained spot in loose, moderately rich soil. Give them a light feeding in the spring when new growth is beginning. Avoid overfertilizing, especially with a nitrogenous fertilizer as that is another reason for poor bloom.

Oriental poppies die back to the ground in midsummer (they do not thrive in hot areas where nights do not cool

74

off), but then new leaf growth will come up which will last through the winter. Apply a loose mulch to the new leaves after the ground is frozen.

POPPY, WELSH-

I have tried to grow Welsh-poppies from seed in my garden in Pennsylvania with no success. I have heard they are difficult to grow and I wonder if you can tell me why?

Welsh-poppies (*Meconopsis cambrica*) do best where summers are cool and moist. In hot summer inland areas, success is doubtful. These plants grow their best in the Pacific Northwest where some species are native. If you can find a cool, moist, partially shaded spot, try the seeds of *M. cambrica*. Seeds should be sown in the fall in pots of sandy loam with peat or leaf mold added. Transplant to 2 inches apart when the second set of leaves has formed. They must be kept in a shaded cold frame all during the growing period and planted out in the spring being careful not to disturb the roots when you move them. The soil in the flower bed should also be sandy and slightly acid.

PRIMROSE

I understand primroses are very difficult to grow, but I would like to try my hand at them. Can you make any recommendations?

Primroses are available in a vast range of species and hybrids ranging from tender to hardy; annual, biennial, and perennial. Some may be grown as house plants in the North. Most require rich, moist (some need actual bog conditions), alkaline soils; cool summers; and partial shade for best growth.

It is impossible to investigate all the types grown in the

short space available here. The English primroses (*Primula vulgaris*) and the Polyantha (*P.* x *polyantha*) varieties are the hardiest and easiest to grow. They are at their best in the shade of tall deciduous trees where they will get spring sun. Keep them watered during dry periods. A mulch is necessary both for moisture retention and as protection against winter cold or dry summer heat.

Primrose fanciers become avid in their pursuit of new acquisitions and it is a highly specialized hobby. If you wish to pursue it in depth, I think it best you look these plants up in a good garden encyclopedia at your library in order to get some idea of the range of plants available for specific conditions and type of flowers.

5

Bulbs for Bloom from Snow to Summer

A most obliging group of garden plants are those grown from bulbs (actually a loose term applied to corms, tubers, rhizomes, and roots). One of the many pleasures of growing them is that some multiply readily, so that a small initial purchase can, in time, lead to a large planting. These bulbous plants have few problems and, providing a few cultural needs are observed, are free-flowering. Since they come in all sizes, they present material suitable for every garden from the tiny winter aconite to the stately lilies. The earliest blooming ones are the first to herald the imminence of spring in northern gardens.

Most require nothing special in the way of soil and will grow and flower in any decent garden soil. Their one major nemesis (besides burrowing rodents) is poor drainage. All of these fleshy bulbs or roots will rot if they stand in water. Fortunately few gardens suffer from totally waterlogged conditions.

A word on buying bulbs. The most important thing to consider is the quality of the bulbs. Don't buy bargain bulbs—especially by mail when you can't see them. Order by mail only from reputable firms. It's all right to buy bargains at your local garden center where they may be on sale because the season is drawing to a close and the garden center is anxious to make room for new material.

Cannas are tender bulbs. Plant them outdoors only after the weather is warm in the spring. They will bloom from early summer until frost. (McDonald/Mulligan)

Examine bulbs carefully as you buy them. Good bulbs should be firm, tubers hard, scaly bulbs should have the scales pressed firmly around them. Look for injuries— damaged surfaces may lead to rot when they are planted. See if bulb bases are free of rot or evidence of fungal disease. Especially in buying begonia tubers, sniff them for evidence of mold.

Keep in mind in planting bulbs that although shade is not a problem since many of the early flowering ones appear before deciduous trees have leafed out, they do need to mature their foliage. Dense shade will not produce good results. As is explained in the answers on pages 86 and 104, the bulbs are fed for next season's growth by the ripening foliage left after the bulb blooms. If you want to have flowers next year, that foliage must be left until it dies down.

Many of the "minor" bulbs have not been covered in the following pages. This is probably due to the fact that they flower so readily and reliably that no questions need be asked about them.

BEGONIA, TUBEROUS

I see a great many potted tuberous begonias set out on the shady sides of houses here in Maine, but I have never seen any growing in flower beds. I would like to plant some in among my perennials instead of the usual annuals. What is the procedure for doing this?

There is no reason why tuberous begonias cannot be grown in flower beds. I have done so successfully. The major drawback in using them to replace annuals among a bed of perennials is that such planting beds are apt to be in full sun and begonias require more shade. However, if your part of Maine is cool in summer, they can take more direct sun than they would in a warmer climate. Also they need a somewhat more acid soil and more moisture than most perennials. For this reason it is best to group them rather than to scatter them through the bed so they can be given special attention. Mine were planted at the front of a bed of day-lilies, which also require less sun than most perennials, so they were compatible. The bed faced northeast where there was sun from dawn till midmorning and then the "high shade" that is right for these exquisite begonias.

Start the tubers indoors in March in flats filled with 3 inches of moistened peat moss. Press the tubers into the peat until their sides are just below the rooting medium. The concave side of the tuber is, of course, at the top and is not covered. Water from the bottom to avoid getting water into the top of the tuber. Keep the peat uniformly moist but not soggy. The tubers should be in good light, but not direct sun, in a cool room.

When there are two good leaves, transplant them to individual 4-inch peat pots. At this time, the tuber can be covered with potting soil. You can make a potting mixture of two parts good loam, one part peat or sphagnum moss, one part compost or rotted manure, and a sprinkling of sand. An alternate potting mixture is to purchase African violet soil and add peat moss and sand.

If you have a cold frame, set them out in that about a week after transplanting to harden them off. Otherwise move them out to a sheltered spot on a porch each day and bring them in at night till all danger of frost is past. They can then be planted out into the bed, still in their peat pots, setting them so that the tuber is covered by 2 inches of soil and they are 12 inches apart.

They need to have had the bed prepared by digging in oak leaf mold, peat moss, well-rotted manure, or other soil-retaining material, plus a sprinkling of cotton seed meal. The bed needn't be deeply dug since they are surface-rooting plants. Mulch around the plants with compost or shredded oak leaves, chopped seaweed, or another acid-type mulch. Keep the soil moist, and during warm, dry periods mist them in the morning.

When flower buds appear, begin fertilizing every two weeks with a weak manure tea or other liquid fertilizer. Six weeks before the average frost date for your area, stop using fertilizer. When the plants stop blooming, they need not be watered as frequently as before.

When frost cuts them down, dig the tubers and put them in a frost-free place until the stalks wilt and can be snapped off at the base. Shake off excess soil and let the tubers sun dry for a few hours. Then store in dry sand or peat moss in a cool place till it is time to restart them next year.

CROCUS

We live in an area where there is abundant native wildlife and we have a lot of trouble maintaining plantings of crocus. Rabbits eat the flowers and leaves, as do deer. I suspect mice and chipmunks eat the corms. Is there any solution to this problem that does not involve setting out poisons?

You might try scattering mothballs around your crocuses as they emerge in the spring, but these repellants seem to be effective for only a short period. Used too liberally they will damage the crocuses. Dried blood meal sprinkled around the plants after each rain is more effective. There are also commercial preparations, such as Chaperone, available. I had a choice planting of double white crocuses which proved so delectable that they were eaten down to the ground systematically every year until they ceased to produce flowers. I seem to have better luck with the less exotic varieties, and more of them have survived.

Deeper planting than is normally recommended for these little corms is also supposed to be somewhat effective against the depredations of mice and squirrels. Try setting them with the tops 4 inches below the soil. Burrowing rodents also dislike digging through sharp gritty material, so a trowelful of grit around the corms might also be a help.

Since our two kittens grew into a pair of enormous cats who are very efficient in patrolling our grounds, we frequently find gifts of mice, moles, and shrews lined up on the doorstep. They may account for the better survival rate of more recent plantings.

Crocuses planted on the northwest side of our house send up a lot of flowers buds early each spring, but the buds do not seem to open very well. How can we get them to open?

It sounds to me as though your crocuses are planted in a spot too shady for them. Crocuses need a lot of sunlight to open their flowers fully. Even crocuses planted in open sunny areas can be observed to keep their blooms tightly

*Crocus like these bloom in early spring from bulbs planted about 2
inches deep the previous autumn. Other "little" bulbs to plant at the
same time include grape-hyacinth,* Anemone blanda, *chionodoxa,
eranthis, galanthus,* Iris reticulata, *puschkinia, and scilla. (The Netherlands Flower-Bulb Institute)*

shut on cloudy overcast days. I think the best thing for you
to do is try to replant the corms next fall in a location more
to their liking.

**My husband and I were going to naturalize several
hundred crocuses in the lawn for spring bloom but have
been told that if we do, we cannot mow the lawn after the
flowers have faded. I do not like the thought of having a
straggly looking lawn. Is this true?**

As with most bulbs, corms, and tubers, the success of next year's flowers depends on the foliage being able to mature (see daffodils on page 86, tulips on page 104). However, the problem is not so bad with crocuses. First of all, they bloom so early in the spring that the lawn has not really gotten off to a good start. Then, perhaps because the corms are so small, it is not necessary to wait until the leaves die back entirely as with most other bulbous plants. They can be mowed after a few weeks and before the foliage begins to wither.

DAFFODILS

Last spring when the daffodils bloomed, I noted several clumps that were not blooming. I assumed this was because they were old plantings that had become overcrowded. I dug them to find this was indeed the case and many small new bulbs had formed in the clumps. I carefully separated the bulbs and immediately replanted them. However, this spring these new plantings produced few and small flowers and fewer plants than I know there were bulbs planted.

By and large, bulbs lifted and stored for the summer in a cool, airy place where they can dry out before dividing and replanting in the fall are more successful than those replanted immediately. It is inevitable in working with fresh bulbs that some injuries occur. When the bulbs are allowed to dry out some of these injuries heal themselves; but when they are replanted immediately, especially in warm parts of the country, it is easier for these spots to rot, leading to the loss of the entire bulb. Replanting bulbs directly after digging is more successful in areas where summer heat is not intense or where the ground is kept cool by the leafy shade of deciduous trees.

Of course, some of your problem may be simply that smaller bulbs you replanted were immature and need time to grow into larger bulbs that will produce full-size flowers.

Daffodils were naturalized in a portion of our lawn some distance from the house so that the leaves could be allowed to die back naturally. The leaves were not mowed down, yet in the second and third spring after planting, bloom is sparse. It does not seem they could have become overcrowded in so short a time.

Lawns are sometimes not ideal places for daffodil plantings. What I suspect has gone wrong with your bulbs is overfeeding from a nitrogenous lawn fertilizer. If you are managing your lawn properly, you are probably feeding it in spring and early fall. It is the fall feeding that is the culprit. The excess nitrogen at the time the bulb is preparing to go dormant causes it to produce excessive late growth so that it does not have a chance to harden off properly before the winter.

A naturalized planting of daffodils at the edge of open woodland has been an early spring pleasure for years. However, last year only a few flowers came up and this year none at all. Full-growing clumps of daffodil foliage show they are still there. What can be wrong?

Your daffodil bulbs have obviously become crowded and need to be lifted and divided. Daffodil bulbs form small offsets which in time grow into new bulbs. After several years these newly formed bulbs crowd each other so that they cannot bloom. By digging the bulbs every few years and replanting them, you will keep your daffodils blooming and acquire more bulbs for larger plantings.

When the daffodil foliage has begun to yellow, but before it falls off, dig a clump up carefully using a spading fork. If you wait till the foliage has come off, you may have difficulty locating the bulbs and may injure some of them as you dig. Let them dry, out of the sun, for a few days. By then the many new, small bulbs will come apart easily without injuring the base from which the roots grow. Discard the tiny ones and keep only those of some size.

You may replant the bulbs directly, especially if you live in a cool climate. Otherwise sort them by size, label them, and store them in a cool airy place for the summer. Replant

84

the bulbs in the fall at the proper time for your region.

Planting proceeds as with new bulbs, except for smaller ones which you may want to plant in an out of the way bed until they mature.

The general rule for planting bulbs is to set them two to three times their depth below the soil surface, measuring from the top of the bulb. For large daffodil bulbs, a depth of 4 or 5 inches and 6 to 8 inches apart is usually recommended. For medium bulbs, 3 or 4 inches and 5 or 6 inches apart. For the tiny ones, 2 or 3 inches below the soil and 3 inches apart.

The soil beneath the bulbs into which the roots grow is where the fertilizer should be placed. Bone meal is the best fertilizer for bulbs. If the soil needs improving, dig in compost or peat as well as the bone meal. Do not use manure

At the present time, there are more than 10,000 different daffodils from which to choose. Plant the bulbs in early fall. (The Netherlands Flower-Bulb Institute)

where it will be in contact with the bulb as it tends to cause the bulb to rot. Well-rotted or dehydrated manure may be dug in a couple of inches below where the bulb will rest.

As with all bulbs, a well-drained site should be chosen. Pockets of soil where water collects, especially in the fall, will also cause bulbs to rot.

We naturalized some daffodil bulbs in the lawn a couple of years ago. They bloomed nicely the first spring, but the next year all we got were some straggly leaves.

I suspect the reason your daffodils did not bloom the second year was that your lawn was mowed and the daffodil leaves with it. The daffodil bulb gets its nourishment for next year's flower production from the leaves which function like little factories sending nutriment down to the bulb. The effort of flowering depletes the bulb. When these leaves are cut off without being allowed to mature and die back naturally, they do not serve their natural part of the growing cycle. The bulb in turn lacks the wherewithal to produce a new flower.

The lawn must be mowed around the maturing leaves until they have died a natural death. If you find this unsightly, you would be wise to dig up the daffodils and replant them where the leaves are not in the way.

DAHLIAS

Can you tell me please how to get the most flowers from my dahlias?

To do their best dahlia plants should be planted where they will get full sun and where the drainage is good. The soil should be prepared (see planting information on page 88) in advance.

Dahlias are thirsty plants and should never be allowed to go dry. If they do, the stalks will harden and they will cease to bloom for the season. As they grow the small plants should be cultivated to prevent weeds from smothering them. When the plant stalk is about a foot tall, pinch out the growing tip. This will cause branching stems to appear. Tie tall plants to stakes as needed.

About mid-July, fertilizing should begin. Either cultivate a side dressing of bone meal and dehydrated cow manure into the soil, or feed every two weeks with a dilute plant food. At this time it is imperative to mulch the plants, both to conserve moisture and to keep weeds from vying with them for moisture and nourishment. Compost, grass clippings, or any loose mulching material will do. If flower buds appear before the plant is of good size, cut them off. Once the plant is full size, larger flowers may be obtained by pinching off the two side buds in each group of three. Be sure to keep faded flowers picked.

Dahlias grown for exhibition purposes are kept to a single main stem, but these are rather ungainly for garden purposes.

Last year I grew dahlias for the first time. I knew the roots could be dug and saved for another year. I kept them in plastic bags in my cool cellar and replanted them this year. The plants did not bloom as profusely as they did last year. Should these roots be discarded and new ones purchased each year?

No, dahlia tubers should not be discarded. They can be kept to produce flowering plants for years to come. From what you say it sounds as though you did not divide the tuberous roots but planted the whole clump. I suspect this accounts for the poor performance of your dahlias this year. Also, storing in plastic bags without some covering medium may have allowed for some drying of the roots before planting. The following is a good way to handle dahlia roots from digging to replanting.

After the tops have been killed by frost in the fall, let a few days go by to allow the roots to ripen. (Unless heavy frost is predicted, in which case dig at once.) Then cut off the tops so about 4 to 6 inches remain. Dig the plants carefully with a spading fork and shake as much soil off as you can. Upend the clump so moisture can drain from the stalks and let them sit in sun until they are dry. Be sure to label the plants as you dig them, if you have grown several varieties, so that you will know what you are setting out next year.

There are many methods of storing dahlia roots. The aim is to keep the dormant tubers cool so growth does not start, yet retain enough moisture so they do not shrivel. Most often these roots are stored in boxes and covered with sand, ashes, or peat. Plastic bags, with some holes punched for air, will work providing the roots are also covered with sand and the like.

They are not planted out in the spring until the soil is warm and all danger of frost is past. Before planting time, they can be given a head start by putting them in flats and partially covering them with damp peat moss. This will also start them growing and facilitate finding the strongest buds. Leave them in the flats only a week or ten days. Each root that has a strong pink bud should be cut from the clump with a piece of the old stalk attached. Growth actually comes from the neck of the root.

Although dahlias are not fussy about soil, obviously well-prepared soil will produce stronger plants and better bloom. Choose a planting site in full sun and with good drainage. Dig a hole about 12 inches wide and 8 inches deep. Put well-rotted manure, compost, or peat at the bottom of the hole and dig it into the subsoil. Mix compost, or peat, and bone meal or other fertilizer into the soil dug from the hole. Put about 2 inches of prepared soil back into the hole. If you are planting large varieties, drive a stake at the back of the hole at this juncture. Lay the root in the hole (which is now about 6 inches deep) with the bud upward nearest the stake. Cover with about 2 inches of prepared soil. As the shoots begin to grow, gradually fill the hole until it is level with the surrounding soil. This is so the heat of the sun can reach the root. If you are planting late when the soil is thoroughly warm, you can fill the hole in directly. Large dahlias should be planted 3 feet apart, dwarf varieties need about 18 inches of spacing between plants.

I have heard that it is possible to increase a favorite dahlia by cuttings as well as root division. How is this done?

In early spring, take the tuberous roots out of their winter storage material and put them in deep flats. Partially cover them with a mixture of moist sand and peat moss and put them into a cool sunny greenhouse or cold frame free from frost. New shoots will soon begin to grow. When there are three nodes on the stems, it is time to take cuttings.

In order to produce a tuber from a cutting, the cut must be made immediately below the second node. Other cuttings will function only as annual plants. Remove the lower set of leaves and plant cuttings in flats of sand or vermiculite. These should have bottom heat. When roots have formed, plant each cutting in a 2-inch pot filled with a mixture of loam, sand, and leaf mold. If they grow too big for their pots before the weather has warmed up enough to plant them where they are to grow, move them into 5-inch pots. When planting them in the garden bed, set the plants an inch or two lower than they were growing in the pots. The old tubers may then be divided and planted as you normally would. The side shoots that remain on the tubers where the cuttings were made can be left on the tuber. Handle carefully so as not to damage these shoots when planting.

FRITILLARY

When we moved from Nevada to New Jersey, I brought some fritillary bulbs from my garden. They're called mission bells. Care was taken to keep them moist and they were planted as promptly as possible to keep them from drying out, but they did not grow at all. From my recollection, the temperatures in New Jersey seem very much the same and I wonder why they did not work.

I don't know which species of mission bells you brought with you since that is the common name for them in the

West, but western varieties of fritillary do not seem to move eastward well. Despite what may seem similar temperatures and conditions, the eastern winters are colder and there is much more rain and snowfall—too much moisture for the western fritillaries.

FRITILLARY, CHECKERED-LILY

I planted several bulbs of the checkered-lily fritillary in my rock garden last year, but this spring they did not all flower. Can you tell me what might be wrong?

The checkered-lily, also called Guinea-Hen flower and snakeshead (actually *Fritillaria meleagris*), can be slow to establish itself. Sometimes it will take a bulb a year to come into bloom. It is for this reason that the bulbs should be planted under as near ideal conditions as possible (rich, but well-drained soil in partial shade) and then moved only when the planting becomes so crowded that it ceases to bloom. When they are moved, they should be divided and replanted at once so there is no chance for the bulbs to dry out. If planted in beds, they should have a little sharp sand placed around them. Plant them about 4 inches deep, deeper if the soil is light and apt to dry out too quickly.

FRITILLARY, CROWN IMPERIAL

I planted some rather expensive bulbs of a variety of crown imperials (I believe the variety was called *Fritallaria lutea maxima*) with very poor results. I planted them in October and mulched them over the winter with peat moss for protection, but almost none of them came up. The bulbs were from a reputable nursery, so it must have been something I did incorrectly.

Although most of the fritillaries need good moisture (as well as good drainage), the hybrids are especially susceptible to rotting if they are kept too moist. They should be planted in deep, rich soil which has been dug out and prepared to a depth of 12 inches. The bulbs should be planted 6 to 8 inches deep, 12 inches apart and *on their sides* so that water does not collect on the surface and cause rot. In coastal areas where there is fog and much dew, the planting bed should be in full sun.

Peat moss is not the appropriate mulch because it compounds the problem by retaining too much moisture. Loose mulches such as salt hay or evergreen boughs are better choices.

GLADIOLUS

I planted gladiolus this summer at my vacation home on Nantucket but they did not flower well. Can you tell me why? We are not right on the shore so they are protected from salt spray.

I would venture to guess that your soil is sandy and high in aklalinity. While gladiolus will tolerate sandy soil, they do not produce flowers as well as they would if some humus had been dug into the soil. Also, your soil should be tested for its alkalinity. A reading over 7.5 pH is definitely detrimental to gladiolus.

Before you leave your summer home, some time after you have dug your gladiolus, incorporate some leaf mold, rotted manure, compost, or peat into the soil. Then spread seaweed gathered from the shore (wash it under the garden hose to remove as much salt as possible) on the bed.

Next spring when this seaweed has dried, it can be chopped with your spade and dug into the bed to decompose. Do this as far in advance of planting as you can manage it. Or the seaweed can be composted (in a heap with alternate layers of soil) and added to the flower bed when it is ready. I know several successful Maine gardeners who use seaweed as the mainstay of their soil building. Mulch the plants during the growing season and, again, dig the mulch in each fall.

If your soil is excessively alkaline, do not use wood ashes or bone meal. Use cotton seed meal, commercial fertilizer or dehydrated manure until pH of soil is slightly acid.

Unappetizing as it may sound, if you have a fisherman in the family, heads, bones, and other inedible fish scraps composted or dug in away from plant roots are an excellent source of phosphorus for plants.

I am planning to dig my gladiolus corms and saving them to replant. Can you tell me how to go about it?

The proper time to dig gladiolus is when the leaves begin to yellow, about six weeks after blooming, or when late plantings are cut down by the first frosts in cold sections of the country. In frost-free climates, it is when they begin to yellow. Cut the withered foliage back to within 2 inches of the corm and store in a frost-free place where they can air dry for two weeks or so. In cold climates where the foliage had not matured before frost, leave it attached during this period while the bulb cures.

After this time, shake off the soil, separate the old corm and the roots which are below the new corm and discard the old corm and roots. If you wish to keep the little cormels that are growing around the new corm, separate these and store them separately. The new corm is your growing stock for next year. The little cormels can be planted somewhere out of the way till they are of flowering size, which will be at least two years. In cold climates, they too will need to be dug and stored each year. Use paper bags for storage and store corms of the same variety and size together, labeling them accurately.

In the spring, replant the ones of flowering size where they are to grow, in good soil with a pH of 6.0 to 6.5 and fertilize as suggested on page 94. Set them 4 to 6 inches apart (8 inches apart for very tall growing varieties) and 3 to 4 inches deep, deeper in light soil. For a succession of blooms, make successive plantings two weeks apart.

What is the best method to grow gladiolus for arrangements?

The best way to grow gladiolus for cutting purposes is in rows by themselves so they do not leave unsightly bare spots in the garden. You can make a bed somewhere out of the way, or plant some rows in among the vegetable garden. Plant the corms 4 to 6 inches apart in rows 18 inches apart and 3 to 6 inches deep. The depths and planting distances, of course, are based on the sizes of the corms. Stakes can be driven at each end of the rows and cords tied on them for supports. The individual stalks can be tied to the cords with string.

Fertilize the plants before the flower stalk appears (see page 94). Flowers should be cut as soon as the lower floret opens. Beware of overfertilizing. This will cause the stalks to be flabby and the flowers will not last well when cut. Be sure not to cut any of the foliage. If you wish a few leaves to add to the arrangements, leave most of them on the plant to nourish the new corm underground or they will not produce flowers on successive years.

I want to plant some gladiolus and have been looking at the bulbs at my garden center. I find it very confusing. Some of the largest ones seem to be less expensive than the next size. I always thought large size bulbs were better.

Several factors are probably involved in the sizes of the gladiolus corms you have been looking at. As with all bulbous plants, beware of bargains. It is true that usually the larger ones are better but large flat bulbs, which may be less expensive, are old and will not produce the best blooms. The prime bulbs are about 2 inches in diameter and are also high vertically. Those sold as No. 1 and No. 2 are your safest bet. Size, of course, is also governed by the variety; the smaller types will have smaller corms. The most expensive ones will be the newer introductions of named varieties produced by breeders.

I planted several groups of gladiolus for a succession of flowers among a bed of mixed annuals. I prepared the bed

carefully and worked in both dehydrated manure and bone meal. They were planted 3 inches apart and 4 inches deep but flowering was poor and, in general, not successful.

It sounds as though you might have killed your gladiolus with kindness. As with many other cormous and bulbous plants, gladiolus corms should not be in direct contact with fertilizers, particularly manures which are apt to burn them. The fertilizers should be scattered 2 inches below the depth at which the corms will be set, then covered with 2 inches of soil and the corms set on that. As the roots grow they will reach down to the fertilizer for nourishment.

Another method is to enrich the garden soil in the fall with organic material so that it is rich in humus, then no fertilizer is needed at planting time. When there are seven leaves the flower spike is about to emerge. At this time fertilizer is cultivated into the soil a few inches from the plants as side dressing and watered in well. A second application should be made after flowering. Keep the plants deeply watered if necessary during the flowering period. The first feeding encourages bloom, the second will promote the growth of a strong, new corm underground.

The fertilizer may also be applied in liquid form in which case it should be watered in every ten days till the flowers have withered.

HYACINTH

Several groups of hyacinths planted at the front of a large flower bed produced beautiful flowers the first year, less the second and quite small spikes this past year. Is this normal?

Your experience with your hyacinths seems to be a common one. Experts differ on the performance of these lovely fragrant bulbs. Many seem to feel that they should be treated as annuals, or at best, as two-year plants. However, there seems to be some evidence that properly planted, mulched,

Hyacinths bring fragrant bloom to a spring garden either in the ground or in planter boxes (as shown here at the Los Angeles State and County Arboretum in Arcadia, California). (James McNair)

and fertilized beds given care in subsequent years can be made to flower well for a number of years.

Plant the bulbs 5 to 6 inches deep in well-prepared, well-drained soil. Good drainage, essential for the well-being of most bulbs, is even more critical with hyacinths as they are more prone to rot. In heavy, clayey soils hyacinths will not do well and sand and compost or peat must be added to lighten the soil. The soil for a hyacinth bed should be dug 12 inches deep and any hard clumps broken up. Well-rotted manure, or dehydrated manure, bone meal, and peat or compost should be thoroughly worked into the layer below where the bulbs are to be planted. A thin layer of sand should be sifted over this and the bulbs put in place 8 to 9 inches apart. The rest of the soil which has been dug out should have peat moss or compost added (and more sand in heavy soils) and be thoroughly mixed so that it is of a fine consistency, then filled in around and over the bulbs.

When the leaves die back, cultivate bone meal into the soil to feed the maturing bulb underground. In cold areas mulch should be applied during the winter. In the spring, as growth begins, again cultivate around the plants to get rid of weeds and to work in more bone meal or other fertilizer. Some years the flower spikes will be smaller, but they should improve again and the planting should last for years.

If your hyacinths were properly planted, try a regular program of fertilizing as previously mentioned. It should bring them back to larger flowering size.

IRIS

Last summer I planted some bearded iris. They have produced fine foliage but no flowers. They were fed this spring with a 5-10-5 formula. Why have they not bloomed?

You have not told me how you planted your iris rhizomes, but I suspect they were planted too deeply. This is the most common cause of lack of bloom in bearded irises. They should barely be covered with soil and certainly no deeper than 1 inch below the surface in full sun. Some growers recommend facing the rhizomes south with the foliage on the north end as it is the heat of the sun on the rhizome that induces good blooming.

I want to plant irises in my garden but there seem to be so many types and varieties and the conditions for them vary so much that I am totally confused.

Yes, it is a confusing subject since there are over 150 species of irises, some with many varieties. It is almost impossible to advise at long distance without knowing the specifics of your garden and your own preferences.

For instance, crested iris (*Iris cristata*) is a tiny, native charmer in woodlands in your state of Virginia. It grows best in partial shade. All types of bearded irises need sun. Most species of iris need a fair amount of water, but good drainage. Many will tolerate dry periods after flowering. None can take water standing about them during cold weather though some—Japanese and Louisiana iris, for instance—actually need flooding at blooming time.

A neutral soil is desirable for most species, but some like a slightly alkaline soil better, others slightly acid. While most species are hardy all over the country, others thrive best in special areas.

I would advise a trip to your local library where you can study one of the good garden encyclopedias for varieties best suited to your location and needs. You can then see what is available at local garden centers or order from one of the good mail-order houses. (See list of mail-order houses at back of book.)

While showing the garden of our newly acquired house to a friend, we stopped to admire a bed of irises in bloom. She told me I would have to dig them up after blooming and replant them in the fall. Since then other friends have told me irises should not be dug up. Who is right?

Whether irises are dug and replanted yearly or not depends on what kind of iris they are. The irises most often seen in gardens are varieties that grow from an elongated root known as a rhizome. One species, the vesper iris, has fibrous roots like a perennial. There are, however, bulbous species called Dutch, Spanish, and English irises.

These bulbous ones are most often grown in southern California where the conditions are just right for them. In other parts of the country the plants do better if the bulbs are dug when the leaves die back and replanted as tulips are (see page 104). The foliage of these tends to be more grasslike than the familiar fan of flat sword shaped leaves. Try digging one up after flowering to see what sort they are.

My iris bed is producing fewer blossoms each year. I am told the bulbs are overcrowded and need dividing. Can you tell me how to go about this?

Yes, every few years iris plantings become crowded and need to be renewed. The best time to do this is after the flowers have stopped blooming. It is possible to carry out the procedure later, but be sure it is done in time to allow the newly planted rhizomes to establish their roots before winter, especially in colder parts of the country.

Lift the whole clump with a spading fork. Discard the old rhizomes and chose those with vigorous new shoots. Each segment should have its own fan of leaves and a growth of stout, healthy roots. Discard shriveled rhizomes and dead leaves, cut off damaged roots and cut the fan of leaves back to 4 to 8 inches depending on size of variety involved.

Whether you are replanting them in the same bed, or moving them to a new bed (which ideally should have been previously prepared), the ground should be deeply worked with well-rotted manure, compost, or peat, as well as bone meal. A little ground limestone can be worked in too, except for varieties that are acid-loving. Form a little mound in each planting hole so that the rhizome rests close to the surface but the roots are allowed to spread down into the soil on each side. Then fill in so that less than an inch of soil is covering the rhizome. In heavy soil it can be set so the fan end of the rhizome is actually sticking out of the ground. In cold climates face the rhizome to the south with the fan of leaves at the upper end. Otherwise space them 6 to 8 inches apart in clumps with the growing tip facing away from the clump. The new growth will be formed out from the tip of the rhizome.

In cold parts of the country it may be necessary to mulch the plantings the first year to avoid heaving before the roots have taken hold. Use compost or shredded leaves, salt hay, or any loose material that will not retain too much moisture. Moisture-retaining materials such as peat may cause the roots to rot.

LILY

I planted some bulbs of regal lily, which is supposed to be an easy-to-grow kind, last fall, but the performance this summer has been poor and they have not flowered well. What can be wrong?

If the roots of your regal lilies (*Lilium regale*) were injured when they were dug or improperly handled so that they dried out before they reached you, this would result in a lack of flowering. But sometimes it just takes a while for lilies to become established, so lack of bloom the first year should not be cause for concern if the foliage is healthy.

I would like to do an extensive planting of lilies. They are such beautiful flowers. Can you give me information on their cultural needs?

Lilies are indeed one of the most exciting of flowers to grow. They are also beset by some of the worst problems known to gardeners. They are subject to mosaic, virus diseases, botrytis, to name a few. Consequently the most important rule to observe is to be sure to buy your bulbs from a lily specialist or from a reputable mail-order house to avoid buying diseased bulbs. (See list of sources at back of book.) Be sure, too, to buy varieties that are disease-resistant.

Prepare the bed well in advance of buying the bulbs as they must be planted immediately after receiving them. Lily roots are severely injured by drying. It would be worth your while to order several catalogs so you can study the varieties and decide which you want.

Many lilies prefer full sun, but most need partial shade. In foggy coastal areas planting in full sun is more desirable. Drainage must be excellent, for although lilies need a lot of moisture, they do not relish standing in water. If drainage is a problem, the easiest thing to do is make a raised bed to insure that the drainage will be good. Watering should be done deeply during dry periods, preferably with a soaker to avoid getting water on the foliage.

Hardy lilies grow from bulbs best planted in the fall or early spring in humusy, well-drained, moist soil. By careful selection from the catalogs, you can have lilies in bloom from June until September. These are "Sunburst" hybrids. (Oregon Bulb Farms)

The soil should be deeply prepared because lilies send their roots down deep. Dig the soil to a depth of 12 inches and improve it with the addition of compost, rotted manure, leaf mold, sawdust, or peat. If your soil is heavy or clayey, lighten it with sand or gritty material. If you are in an area troubled with mice, gophers, or other rodents, it would be well to use wire baskets to plant the bulbs in. Garden centers carry these. Or you may line the sides of the bed with hardware cloth as described under tulips on page 104. Bone meal and fish meal or a chemical fertilizer should be mixed in the soil at planting time. It should be low in nitrogen and high in phosphorus and potash (such as 5-10-8). Wood ashes are fine for adding potash unless the soil is already too alkaline. Lilies need a nearly neutral pH (6.0 to 6.4), although most tolerate a somewhat acid soil. Some do prefer a slightly alkaline one (around 7.0). Because of these variations, it is a good idea to have the hybrids or species chosen in advance so you will know how to meet their needs. You will also need to know the colors and periods of bloom for your part of the country, and the heights to which they grow in order to plan the bed effectively.

Lilies need to have their roots kept cool and many need to have the lower portion of their stems in shade. In mixed plantings this is accomplished by the shade cast by the other perennials. You can also plant annuals at the front of the bed. In addition, a mulch of shredded leaves, buckwheat hulls, sawdust, or similar material must be provided.

The depth at which bulbs are set varies with the kind. Basal rooting ones, that is ones where the roots grow from the bottom of the bulb, should be covered by 2 or 3 inches of soil (except for the madonna lily [*Lilium candidum*], which should only be 1 or 2 inches below the soil surface). Most lilies fall into the stem-rooting category; that is, they produce roots along the portion of the stem that is below ground, as well as from the base of the bulb. These need to be planted two or three times the depth of the bulb below the soil surface. Small varieties can be spaced 6 inches apart, larger ones as much as 12.

Lilies whose roots are injured at planting time will not bloom. Basal rot resulting from poor drainage will also impede flowering. But sometimes it just takes a while for the bulbs to establish themselves, so lack of bloom the first year should not be cause for concern if the foliage is healthy.

Cutting flowers for indoor use, unless very little stem is taken, also will injure the bulb. The stems should be left to ripen on the plants, only being cut back somewhat as they wither. At least a foot of stump should be left at the end of the flowering season to be pulled off in early spring. The faded flower head should, of course, be cut off before seeds form.

RANUNCULUS, TURBAN

I have tried to grow turban ranunculus in my garden in New Jersey but nothing came up. Then I started them in a pot in the basement in early spring and moved the pot outdoors as soon as the weather was frost-free. All the tubers germinated but only one bloomed. Is there any way to be more successful with these lovely flowers? I am especially fond of them.

I share your fondness for turban ranunculus (a hybrid of *Ranunculus asiaticus*), also called Persian ranunculus, and think it is one of the prettiest flowers around. Unfortunately these hybrids can only be grown outdoors where climates are mild. In areas where winters are cool but above freezing they are planted from November to February. Ranunculus are not tolerant of heat either and what probably happened to the ones you potted up was that the weather got too hot for them. They do very well in a cool greenhouse where nighttime temperatures are below 50°F.

If you have a cold frame, you might try your hand at them again. Plant them in a bed or in pots surrounded by peat moss in the cold frame in the fall. They should be spaced 6 inches apart in a bed, 2 inches in pots, and 2 inches deep. Plant them claws down in rich soil with added compost and sand. Bone meal should also be mixed into the soil. Keep the soil evenly moist. When the temperature drops below freezing, cover the frame to keep the interior temperature of the cold frame above freezing. On days when the weather is above freezing, raise the cover so that air may circulate. They should bloom in April, well ahead of hot summer months.

Puschkinia, like the crocus, is considered one of the minor or "little" spring-flowered bulbs. Plant it in autumn in sunny, well-drained soil. (The Netherlands Flower-Bulb Institute)

TULIP

My husband and I have retired to Florida and I am told tulips, which I love, won't do well here. Is this true?

It used to be true. Under ordinary temperature conditions in southern Florida, tulips won't grow. Tulips need a period of 40°F. (or less) temperature. But now many garden centers in southern states sell specially cold-treated bulbs for southern planting. If not, then with a little extra trouble you can cold treat your own. Since 40° is the average refrigerator temperature, buy tulip bulbs whenever they are available in fall catalogs and store them in your refrigerator until planting time. A minimum of six weeks of cold is necessary.

If you wish to keep the bulbs for another season's bloom, after flowering let the foliage mature to feed the bulb. (Be sure to snip off flowers as they fade so they do not go to seed.) Dig the bulbs, and keep them in a dark dry place. If you have several varieties, be sure you keep them separate and labeled so you know which you are replanting. Around September return them to the refrigerator. Replant as before.

Last fall I put in a number of species tulips at the edge of the woodland that adjoins our lawn. I thought they would be charming. But this spring nothing at all appeared. What could have happened to them?

What probably happened to your species tulips is that mice, moles, or some other species of rodent got to the bulbs and ate them. In a country setting you would be wise to plant the bulbs in wire baskets. These are available at garden centers. You can also make your own protective barrier out of ¼-inch metal mesh called hardware cloth. Dig the planting hole a few inches deeper than you need to plant the bulbs and lay a square of hardware cloth in the bottom. Frame the sides of the planting hole with more hardware cloth so that it extends 2 inches above the soil surface. Put several inches of good garden soil or compost fertilized with bone meal in

104

Tulips, the bulbs of which can be planted any time in the fall, right up until the ground freezes, make the best show if they are massed in clumps of ten or more of the same variety. Here they bloom in the company of wallflower, a biennial. (The Netherlands Flower-Bulb Institute)

For best results, plant tulip bulbs in soil that has first been deeply spaded; if it is dry and hard, or soggy and wet, incorporate quantities of sand and sphagnum peat moss, then proceed with planting. Bone meal is an excellent organic fertilizer for all bulbs. (The Netherlands Flower-Bulb Institute)

the hole, then set the bulbs in place. Six or eight tulips can be planted in each. Fill the hole in and fit another piece of hardware cloth over the top. When growth starts in the spring, remove this surface hardware cloth. Cultivate some bone meal into the soil.

I had this very same experience and I turned to a simpler solution. I gave up the idea of naturalized tulips and planted miniature daffodils and windflowers (*Anemone blanda*). Mice do not seem to be fond of them.

We planted a beautiful tulip bed last fall and this spring it was a glory. Neighbors tell us that next year the size of the flowers will be smaller, that in order to have tulips at peak bloom they should be treated as annuals and the bulbs discarded each year and new ones replanted in the fall.

If you must have the largest tulip flowers possible, then yes, this is the way to handle tulips. However, by and large, the average tulip bed will bear flowers of respectable size for three years at least. After that most do get noticeably

Tulips are excellent for planting in pockets in-between foundation plantings of shrubs and evergreens. By carefully selecting varieties from the catalogs, you can have tulip bloom spread over a period of several weeks—from early spring to the beginning of summer. (The Netherlands Flower-Bulb Institute)

smaller. Tulips can be made to bear larger flowers longer with deep planting. It is usually recommended that 5 or 6 inches of soil cover the bulbs (measuring from the top of the bulb). By setting them so the tops are 8 to 12 inches below the surface, you will get more years of enjoyment.

You will need to spade the soil to a depth of 12 to 18 inches in a spot where the drainage is good. The soil beneath the bulbs should be well prepared with compost or peat and bone meal since it is from the soil beneath them that tulip roots get their nourishment. Each year, after flowering, tulip bulbs renew themselves entirely—that is, a whole new bulb and root system is formed for the following year's growth nourished by the ripening foliage. As a rule several smaller bulbs are formed, resulting in smaller flowers. With deep planting, fewer small offsets are formed.

Feeding the bulbs well will also produce better results. Cultivate bone meal into the soil around the tulips after the flowers fade and again in the spring when growth starts. Keep faded flowers picked, both to cut down the drain of energy on the plant and as a disease-prevention measure. It is thought that fallen petals encourage the spread of botrytis to which tulips are prone.

Another method of handling a tulip bed, but one involving a lot of work, is to dig up your bed yearly after foliage has yellowed, discarding the smallest bulbs. Handle as recommended for southern planting on page 104. According to the correct planting time for tulip bulbs in your area, back-time the refrigerator storage so they have at least six weeks of cold before planting.

Winter Aconite

Some tiny bulbs of winter aconite purchased at my gardening center last fall failed to come up and flower. Is it possible that the bulbs were not good?

The little bulbs (properly tubers) of winter aconite (*Eranthis hyemalis*) have a reputation for being hard to start. They are

Bougainvillea is a vine that can be grown outdoors all year only in frost-free climates. Elsewhere it can be cultivated as a container plant and wintered over indoors in a sunny window or greenhouse. (Mc-Donald/Mulligan)

BOUGAINVILLEA

I live in Yuma, Arizona, and have been thrilled to see bougainvillea growing in California. Would it work here? How should I grow it?

Bougainvillea might do well in your location, especially if it is grown against a sheltered sunny wall. These vines need a good soil with sand and gritty material added for fast drainage.

Before planting, string wires on the wall where you want to train the vine and tie up the shoots as they grow. The roots of bougainvillea do not bind the soil into a tight root ball as do most plants, and you must be careful in planting

111

to not disturb the soil in which it is growing. Put the plant as it comes from the nursery, pot and all, in its planting hole. Slit the sides of the container so that they can be removed. The bottom of the container can be left in the ground to rot away.

Although bougainvillea will tolerate drought conditions, during the growing season it should be kept well watered.

To promote flowering, the side shoots should be trimmed back so only two buds remain. This should be done in early spring after danger of frost is past.

CLEMATIS

My clematis "Belle of Woking" does not bloom although I fertilize it in the spring and prune it in the fall. What can I do to make it bloom?

Your "Belle of Woking" is one of the varieties of clematis that flowers on old wood formed the previous year. Radical pruning in the fall removes the branches which would provide the following year's blossoms. This variety should be pruned lightly after blooming, and further pruning in fall or early spring should only be to remove spindly or damaged growth. Varieties of *C.* x *jackmanii,* such as "Mrs. Cholmondeley" can be pruned severely in the fall or early spring as buds start to grow since the flowering sepals bloom in summer on growth produced that season.

Varieties of clematis fall into three major groups: those that flower in the spring; those that flower in the spring and bear a second crop in summer; and those that flower only in summer. The first type produces flowers on old wood, the second makes its spring show from old wood then produces new wood for a second blooming, and the third kind only blooms on new growth.

My lovely clematis, "Comtesse de Bouchaud" does poorly. It is rangey and flowers are not produced lavishly as I thought they would be. How can I improve the flowering?

Sweet autumn clematis bears clusters of white flowers late in the season. It is one of the most easily cultivated and rewarding of the perennial vines. (J. Horace McFarland Company)

"Comtesse de Bouchaud" is one of the most free-flowering varieties of clematis and yours must have several problems if it is not blooming well. First of all, this is one of the varieties that blossoms on growth made the same season (see previous answer). When it is young it should be cut back to at least a foot from the ground. When it is two or three years old and the basal stems are thicker, 2 feet is about the right height to allow it to remain. If yours is an older plant that was not pruned properly its first three years, then it cannot be cut so severely now and you will have to use your judgment about how far back to prune it. This pruning can be done in the fall, or better yet, in the spring when buds begin to swell.

Hybrid clematis like this one bloom off and on from June until frost. Train them on a low fence or as high as you like on a wall-mounted trellis. For best results, shade the roots in moist soil, but allow sun to reach the vine itself. (McDonald/Mulligan)

Wood trellises like these are perfect for training clematis and other vines on a wall. The Paris daisy in the foreground is a tender perennial, the same as the geranium. (Maynard Parker)

114

Amaryllis (right) grows from a bulb and makes a spec-tacular flowering house plant.

Rex begonias (left) are grown for their showy foliage; cane-types (right) for their angel-wing leaves and grape-like clusters of hanging flowers.

Bromeliads like this hybrid neoregelia are among the most durable of all exotic house plants.

Christmas cactus needs naturally short days in September and Octo-ber to bloom on schedule.

Waxplant or hoya bears its clusters of waxy, star-shaped, fragrant flowers, only after its roots are pot-bound and there is considerable foliage.

This pink-flowered cineraria (right) needs a sunny, moist, cool (but not freezing) atmosphere in which to bloom.

(Left) Annual sunflower seeds sprout quickly in warm, moist soil and grow to 8-feet tall, crowned by single flowers, or doubles like this one, in one season.

Bleeding-heart or dicentra needs part sun and moist, humusy soil. This form blooms in the spring; the fern-leaf blooms off and on until autumn.

Poppy-flowered anemones can be planted outdoors only in mild winter climates; elsewhere they can be grown in a cool, sunny, airy greenhouse or plant room.

Japanese iris, a hardy perennial, can be depended on to flower each summer if it receives some direct sunlight with moist, rich soil.

Iceland poppies grow easily from seeds. In early spring, broadcast them over an area that will be sunny and moist, but well-drained.

Dahlias (left) grow from tender bulbs planted outdoors after danger of frost in the spring. They bloom from mid-summer until frost.

Miniature roses (right) look exactly the same as normal-size ones; however, the bushes grow only inches tall and the blooms are hardly bigger than a thimble.

Roses like this hybrid grandiflora can be counted on for blooms from June to frost; they need at least a half day of sun, however.

For maximum effect, plant at least ten bulbs of one tulip (this one is lily-flowered) in a clump in early fall for bloom the following spring.

Geraniums like these require full sun, moist soil and a fertilizer low in nitrogen.

Clematis is a beautiful flowering vine. For best growth, situate the roots so that they will be mostly shaded, but with the tops exposed to sun.

Cockscomb, or crested celosia, (right) is one of the annual flowers that may be cut and hung to dry in a shady, airy place, then used in dried bouquets.

Impatiens (left) are among the few flowers that can be counted on for color in the shade during warm weather. Keep the soil moist.

Dwarf French hybrid marigolds, like these growing in an iron cauldron, are ideal choices for summer flowers in an area that is sunny and tends to dryness.

Delphiniums take some special effort in most climates, but for stunning spikes of blue, lavender, purple or white flowers, they are without equal.

Foxglove, or digitalis, is usually treated as a biennial. Its main bloom season occurs in late spring and early summer.

Tuberous begonias grow from a fleshy tuber planted indoors in late winter, then moved outdoors in warm weather. They need moist soil, shade and cool nights.

Hosta (left) is a hardy perennial with handsome foliage all season. The flowers, which appear briefly, are showy and fragrant.

There are also cultural needs that you should look into. The ideal soil in which to plant clematis should be a loose, fast-draining one that is mildly alkaline. Test the soil in which your vine is growing for acidity. If it is acid, correct this by lightly cultivating in some ground limestone. A clematis cannot be moved satisfactorily. If the soil is heavy and claylike, work in some rotted manure and sand. Also, especially if the clematis is in a sunny spot, is there shade in the root area? These vines need what is referred to as a "cool root run." If the ground at the base of your clematis is sunny, provide shade by mulching with stones, compost, or other organic material. Low-growing shrubs can be planted so they will cast a shadow at the base of the clematis.

GLORYBOWER

I have a glorybower vine growing on the west side of my house here in Kentucky, but it does not flower well.

It would be best to move your glorybower (*Clerodendrum thomsoniae*) to a sunnier location. More sun will bring it into better bloom.

HONEYSUCKLE

Can you recommend a vine which is hardy in coastal Maine that can be used to cover an arbor and that blooms all summer? It should also be a low-maintenance vine as I am not able to do much physical work in the garden and do not wish to be saddled with a lot of pruning or pulling suckers.

A trouble-free vine that reliably covers itself with scented flowers all summer and is hardy where you are is everblooming honeysuckle (*Lonicera* x *heckrottii*). The flowers are much more attractive than the usual honeysuckle. They form large clusters and the individual blossoms are purple-red outside, yellow inside, with the familiar honeysuckle scent. They bloom freely from June till frost puts a stop to them. I've grown these midway up the Maine coast only pruning out an occasional dead twig and giving them an annual mulch of compost mixed with bone meal. They are supposed to be subject to aphids, but mine never had any.

HYDRANGEA, CLIMBING

I would like to grow a climbing hydrangea and wonder if it is hardy and will flower in northern Michigan.

Yes, climbing hydrangea (*Hydrangea anomala petiolaris*) should be winter hardy where you are. If it has a tall tree, a stone wall, or other support, it will climb quite freely, clinging with its aerial roots. Without support it will be sprawly. Either way the round, lacy white flowering heads are quite lovely. It is an especially useful vine because it will succeed and bloom in partial shade as well as sun. Give it good soil and adequate moisture—especially if planted in the sun.

JASMINE

Can you tell me of a variety of jasmine that will be winter hardy in southern Pennsylvania? I love the exquisite fragrance of the white flowers and wonder if it is possible to create a sheltered location for it.

Some jasmines are marginally winter hardy as far north as southern New York. The most common is winter jasmine (*Jasminum nudiflorum*); alas, it is neither white nor fragrant. The white-flowered, fragrant kinds such as *J. officinale* are primarily limited to warmer climates. One fragrant species bearing yellow flowers which might work for you in a sheltered spot with winter protection is Italian jasmine (*J. humile*). Give it a sunny location in ordinary garden soil.

117

PASSION-FLOWER

I am growing a passion-flower vine (the tag from the nursery said *Passiflora* x *alato-caerulea*) on a trellis in my garden in southern California, where I have been assured it is hardy. It is making fair growth but not blooming. Why?

I hope your passion flower is planted in a sunny position in good garden soil with excellent drainage. During the growing season the soil must be watered frequently. What your plant probably needs to bring it into bloom is a regular feeding program during the growing season. Use fish emulsion at the rate recommended on the bottle every two or three weeks.

SILVER FLEECE-VINE

I need a tough, fast-growing hardy vine to screen an unsightly storage area in our New York City backyard. I would like it to be flowering and have attractive foliage. It can be deciduous as we only use the outdoor space in summer.

A vine which meets all your requirements (and withstands city pollution) is the silver, or Chinese, fleece-vine (*Polygonum aubertii*). It is a rampant, fast-growing plant with glossy heart-shaped leaves and creamy white flowers that bloom all summer. As a matter of fact, the main problem with silver fleece-vine is that it may take over a small space. Keep it in hand by pruning (even to the ground) in the fall. Water it during dry spells in the summer.

A vine-covered arbor makes an inviting focal point for almost any garden. This one made of roughsawn logs is covered by a grapevine. (Mc-Donald/Mulligan; photographed at the Berkshire Garden Center, Stockbridge, Mass.)

TRUMPET-VINE

When we bought our house there was a rampant old trumpet-vine growing up the screened porch. I cut it back radically to let in some light, but it is so vigorous that it immediately overtook the porch again and had to be pruned once more. It is not flowering, though, and I wonder if it is too old?

Trumpet-vine (*Campsis radicans*) is a very trouble-free rampant grower. Yours is not flowering because of the radical yearly pruning you are giving it. I think you have to make a choice between whether you'd rather have flowers on the vine or light on the porch.

For best flowering, only the side growths should be cut back to two or three buds after the leaves fall.

If you decide it is the wrong plant for the location, dig a few suckers and plant them where they will not be overwhelming, than remove the old plant altogether. These vines are so sturdy that you should not be surprised if after you do all this, a new trumpet creeper develops and grows up your porch. Any bit of root left in the ground may produce a new vine.

VANILLA TRUMPET-VINE

I have heard of a tropical vine that blooms for a long period with trumpet-shaped purple and white flowers that are scented like vanilla. Can I grow it in southern Florida?

The vine you ask about sounds like the vanilla trumpet-vine (*Distictis lactiflora*). It is native to Mexico and grows only where there is no frost. It should be an excellent choice for you. It blooms for nearly eight months at a stretch. The flowers start out purple and gradually fade through lavender to white. It requires only slight pruning to keep it within bounds.

Wisteria is one of the earliest vines to bloom in the spring. It is available in both white and purple forms, as a vine, or trained as a small tree. (Maynard Parker)

121

WISTERIA

My healthy, thriving wisteria vine, trained on a trellis, does not bloom. How can I induce it to bloom?

First of all, I hope that your wisteria was grown from a cutting and not from seed, as the latter may take many years to come into bloom. The usual ones sold at reputable nurseries are grafted, and it is important to keep the suckers that come up from the rootstock from developing. It is customary to let wisteria make free vegetative growth while it is being trained to cover the frame where it is wanted, removing growth that does not fit the space for which it is intended and cutting back straggly growth to half its length. Remove growth that forms on the trunk.

Although wisterias should be planted in good soil, too-rich soil and much feeding will induce excessive vegetative growth at the expense of flowers. It is believed that branches trained horizontally are more floriferous.

Pruning is the key to blooming. Side shoots should be cut back during the summer to induce the formation of next year's flowering spurs. Further pruning should be done in winter. Mulch the vine after the ground freezes in winter. If all this does not produce flowering, try root pruning and feeding as described for lilacs on page 137–139.

Very far north the flowering spurs may be damaged by late spring frosts. The Japanese species (*Wisteria floribunda*) is somewhat hardier than the Chinese one (*W. sinensis*).

122

7

Shrubs for Color
in All Seasons

Shrubs are the prime materials of landscape design. Because of their variety of size and form, they bring an architectural element to the garden. A well-planned bed of shrubs should present an exciting array of shapes and heights, leaf textures and colors, as well as color of bloom.

The time of bloom should be staggered so there is always something flowering during the growing season. In the fall, some shrubs put on a brilliant display of foliage, just as trees do. When the leaves fall, some of them have colored twigs or present an intricate branching silhouette. And, of course, some are evergreen. All these points must be kept in mind if an extensive planting is being made. Again, study up on those that meet your own particular needs and tastes.

In planting shrubs, remember not to place them so close to walls or fences that they will be unable to make balanced growth, or so close together that they will crowd each other as they fill out. If you are planting a new border and feel that allowing room for the eventual spread of the shrubs results in a sparse look, interplant them with less desirable and inexpensive ones so that these can later be cut out. Or plan to transplant some of the shrubs to another location as they grow. Remember, though, that moving a half-grown shrub with a good ball of earth is hard work.

All these elements, plus the flower color and time of bloom, should enter into a carefully planned shrub border. Finally, to me one of the great uses of shrubs is for feeding birds in the fall. There are so many shrubs which, after flowering, produce colorful berries that this should not be overlooked in purchasing new shrubs.

ABELIA

Will you please tell me how to prune abelia for maximum bloom?

As with most flowering shrubs, pruning off tips reduces the amount of flowering wood. One or two branches which have flowered should be cut out at ground level early in the spring to encourage strong new shoots to grow up. New growth will produce flowers more lavishly than older wood. Such pruning also will allow the shrub to develop its naturally graceful arching form. Top growth should be pruned only if it has been killed by low winter temperatures. This may occur where temperatures fall to 10° F.

AZALEA

My wife and I planted a row of evergreen azaleas of the variety "Hinodegiri" to define a backyard terrace area. These azaleas are doing nicely as they are protected from midday sun by tall trees nearby. However, I would like to treat them as a hedge and shear them so they are uniform in size and shape. My wife says they will not bloom if I do this. Is this so?

You can have your cake and eat it with your azalea planting if you are willing to compromise a little. After the shrubs bloom in the spring, shear them lightly to the shape desired. This procedure may be repeated again before August.

Past that time you will remove next year's flower buds. The variety "Hinodegiri" tends to grow rather compactly, so your hedge should retain a relatively tidy appearance. If you follow this procedure, you will find your azaleas will actually bloom more profusely than in previous years. Pinching out the growing tips of evergreen azaleas is recommended to induce more bloom. In essence, this is what your light pruning will do.

BEAUTYBUSH

My three-year-old beautybush has not flowered yet. What can I do to start it blooming?

Beautybush (*Kolkwitzia amabilis*) is a relatively trouble-free shrub, flowering freely. It does though take a few years for one to become established and begin blooming. You can help it along by feeding it this spring. Cultivate bone meal into the soil around it or feed it with another high-phosphate fertilizer.

BLUEBERRY

My highbush blueberries have bloomed and produced fruit lavishly for years. Now they are flowering less and the berries are fewer and smaller. What can I do to restore them?

The first question that comes to mind in answer to your problem is to wonder whether you have been pruning your blueberries regularly. Bushes that are more than three years old require annual pruning. Old plants that have become dense should have one of the old branches in the center of the plant cut out to let in sunlight. Weak twiggy growth, branches that bear few fruits or any that are damaged should also be pruned yearly. This may be done any time after the plants go dormant in the fall and before new growth begins in spring. Damaged portions or poorly fruiting ones can be removed anytime.

I also wonder whether you are maintaining the proper soil acidity which blueberries need. They have the same soil requirements as rhododendrons (see page 140 for maintaining soil acidity).

Although we have a small property and little garden space, I thought it would be fun to have some blueberries. A couple of years ago I bought a two-year highbush blueberry plant which I was told at the nursery would have matured sufficiently to bear fruit the following year. It does bloom and fruit, but I think the yield is rather poor. How can I remedy this? I fertilized it with a special acid fertilizer to no avail.

You do not tell me what variety of blueberry you planted. Most blueberries are self-fertile but produce fruit more abundantly if they are cross-pollinated. Try to find space to tuck in another plant of a different variety close enough for the bees to do their work.

Last spring I planted three highbush blueberries in a corner of my vegetable garden. They didn't do well last year and this year can hardly be called thriving. What did I do wrong?

You don't give me very much information about how you planted your blueberries. Were they one-year rooted cuttings or two-year-old plants? Even the latter could not be expected to bear much fruit the first year. I assume since they are in your vegetable garden that there is full sun, which is as it should be.

If you planted them in your regular garden soil, that could be what went wrong right there. Regular soil for vegetables should be slightly alkaline, although a number of vegetables will tolerate somewhat acid soil. But blueberries must have very acid soil—a pH of 4.0 to 5.2 is generally recommended.

Planting holes 18 inches deep by 2 feet wide should have been dug and at least 50 percent peat added to the soil. If your soil is heavy the mixture could have been two parts peat, one part sand, and one part your garden soil. Cottonseed meal, which is an acid fertilizer, should also have been mixed in.

If you are planning to correct your soil, necessitating digging your plants, be sure to keep a ball of earth on the roots during the move so that they do not dry out. Apply a permanent mulch in the winter, after the ground freezes, of shredded oak leaves, sawdust, or other acid material to maintain the acidity of the soil. Fertilize the shrubs each year with cottonseed meal or aluminum sulphate, or a formula recommended for rhododendrons.

Keep the mulch a few inches back from the stems. If you use a sawdust mulch, in subsequent years when fertilizing, be sure to use a high-nitrogen fertilizer as sawdust frequently causes a nitrogen deficiency. Cottonseed meal is the perfect organic fertilizer for blueberries since it is high in nitrogen and will aid in keeping the soil acid.

Blueberries do not begin to bear well until they are three years old, so whether you planted one- or two-year plants is also a factor in the amount of berries produced.

SPANISH BROOM

A neighbor here in Virginia where I live has several Spanish broom plants which have masses of small yellow flowers all summer long. I admired them so often that she finally suggested I take one for my own garden. We transplanted it very carefully early in the spring. It is planted in full sun but it has not blossomed and is looking poorly. I was told it was not particular as to soil, but perhaps it is.

I can't tell from your description which of the Spanish brooms you acquired from your neighbor—*Spartium junceum* or one of the *Genista* species. However, neither of these transplants successfully after it is mature. You would have done better to take a seedling rather than a full-grown plant. Both plants are so easily raised from seed that it is worth your while to try starting them, particularly if you have a cold frame.

Sow the seeds in early spring in a pot of sterile, sandy loam. When the seedlings begin to crowd the pot and are large enough to transplant, pot each in its own small pot. Repot as necessary, wintering them over in the cold frame, until they are two years old. At that time they can be planted where you want them to grow.

You are right, they're not fussy about soil.

BUTTERFLY-BUSH

How can I get my butterfly-bush to bloom more profusely?

You do not tell me to which species your butterfly-bush belongs. If it flowers in late summer, it is a variety of *Buddleia davidii* which in cold climates may die back to the ground. The roots should be heavily mulched for winter protection. This species flowers on the new growth produced that year and so the shoots should be pruned in the spring to within a few inches of the old stems.

If it blooms in June, it is *B. alternifolia,* called fountain butterfly-bush. Bloom is improved on this species by pruning the blooming shoots off after flowering is past. This will force the formation of new blooming shoots.

CAMELLIA

I purchased a small camellia from a nursery two years ago. It was planted according to their directions and in a sheltered semishaded spot. It has grown somewhat but does not have flowers.

Do you have any idea whether your camellia was grown from seed? Or how old it actually is? I suspect it may be quite a young seedling. It is rare for a camellia grown from seed to flower before it is four years old and more usual for plants to be from five to eight years old before they come into bloom.

We transplanted a beautiful camellia shrub from a friend's garden last year. It seemed to be all right but the buds that formed dropped off before blooming.

You have not given me any information about where your camellia shrub was planted or how. Camellias have very specific needs and there are so many reasons for failure in flowering.

Since it was a large shrub I assume it was moved with care, properly balled and burlapped against the roots drying out, and that it was planted in good, slightly acid soil.

How was it set in the soil? Camellias must not have their feeder roots deeply buried—no more than an inch below soil surface. It is wise in planting a camellia to have it a bit higher than the rest of the bed since it will settle a bit after planting. It should also be sheltered from wind and noonday sun.

Camellias are extremely sensitive to both over- and underwatering. If your plant is situated in a spot where the water does not drain off promptly, this will cause the buds to fall off without blooming. (A hillside often is an ideal spot for a camellia so that there is no problem with water runoff.) If the plant is allowed to go too dry during its blooming season this, too, will cause the buds to drop.

I live in southern Arizona and recently purchased two container-grown camellias for my terrace. They can easily be brought into an unheated porch if we have a cold snap. They bloomed well but I now detect yellowing on some of the leaves although the veins are green. What can be causing this?

It sounds as though your camellias are suffering from chlorosis which is an inability of the plant to take in iron through its roots because of alkaline soil. In many parts of the Southwest the water is excessively alkaline and, as you water your plants, salt deposits are building in the soil. To

129

correct the problem begin by flushing the soil in the plant tubs, even though you will have to use your alkaline water to do this. The flooding will leech out some of the excess salts that have built up in the tubs. Lightly cultivate a little cottonseed meal or aluminum sulphate into the surface soil. When feeding the plants use an acid formula plant food.

Though it is troublesome, since you only have two camellias, it might be worth your while to collect rainwater and use it exclusively to water these plants.

CRAPE-MYRTLE

Can I grow crape-myrtle here in Ohio? I think they are such beautiful shrubs?

Crape-myrtle (*Lagerstroemia indica*) is not supposed to be winter-hardy north of Zone 7 on a U.S. Department of Agriculture map. But one often hears stories of the shrub surviving far out of its range. The reason for this is that the roots are fairly winter-hardy, so that although the top winter kills (as far as the ground during a severe winter), new growth emerges from the roots in the spring. Since crape-myrtle flowers on new wood produced that season, it is possible to have a flowering one even outside its natural climate.

Try a crape-myrtle, planting it in a protected sunny spot in well-drained rich garden soil. In the early winter when the ground freezes, mulch it with salt hay. If you find the top does winter kill, you might try giving it some winter protection. Tie up the branches and cover them with a padding of salt hay as insulation. Then wrap the whole plant in burlap.

FIRETHORN

I would like to grow firethorn at my home in Stamford, Connecticut, and wonder if it is winter-hardy.

The original species of firethorn would probably be marginally hardy in your area, but the newer varieties of *Pyracantha coccinea* are more hardy and also somewhat resistant to fire blight. "Lalandei" seems to be the most satisfactory and the one most commonly available. The white flowers are followed by orange fruits. "Thornless," which has red fruits, and "Kasan," which has orange-red berries, are also good varieties. (See page 168 for control of fire blight.)

FORSYTHIA

Last fall I pruned my forsythia after the leaves had fallen, but this spring there was very little bloom. How can I make the shrub bloom again?

Forsythia should be pruned immediately after blooming. By pruning in the fall you cut off the buds which had formed on the shrub ready to bloom in the spring. Although forsythias may be sheared to shape, this will eventually result in bare wood at the lower part of the shrub. It is wiser to remove one of the old branches down to the ground every three years and prune only those branches which are out of bounds.

HIBISCUS, CHINESE

I was given a potted Chinese hibiscus as a house plant and I have heard they will grow outdoors. Will it grow and bloom outdoors anywhere in the country and, if so, what care does it require?

In most parts of the country Chinese hibiscus (*Hibiscus rosa-sinensis*) must be grown as a house plant. It is suitable for outdoor planting only in the extreme southern portions of the country. Where conditions are right for it, the hibiscus is a fast-growing shrub growing to 15 feet in southern California and central and south Florida, but capable of growing to 30 feet in the tropics. To produce bloom they need heat, sun, and good garden soil. Drainage must be excellent, though they need to be kept well watered and will not survive under drought conditions.

Temperatures must not often drop below 30°F. They will survive an occasional frost, but it is best to plant them in a sheltered location (such as under the protection of a tall tree) if occasional frost is likely where you are. If you are in a marginal area where temperatures do drop for a few days at a stretch, grow them in pots or tubs so they can be taken indoors. In coastal areas they must be sheltered from wind.

See house plant culture of these plants on page 200.

The fuchsia is a tender shrub that can withstand little or no freezing. In cold climates, grow it as a container plant and winter over in any bright, frost-free enclosure; keep the soil on the dry side during this period and do not fertilize. Trim back and start into growth in the spring. (George W. Park Seed Co., Inc.)

HOLLY

We have recently purchased a house in Oregon. We want to relandscape our grounds as they are in bad shape. There are two beautiful English holly shrubs about 7 feet high. Last year one of them was covered with berries while the other had none. We want to move these shrubs to a different location and wonder what is best suited to them so that the other holly will bear fruit.

Most hollies are "dioecious"—that is, plants have either male or female flowers on separate plants. Only the female holly will bear berries, but it will not do so unless there is a male plant nearby for cross-pollination. You obviously have the necessary male and female shrubs. If you want another fruited one, you will have to plant another female plant.

Ilex aquifolium, the English holly, is essentially a tree. It can be kept to shrub size by judicious pruning. The ideal spot for relocating these shrubs is one in sun or partial shade, protected from wind. Transplanting is best done in the fall with early spring a second choice. Before moving the plants, knock off all, or most, of the leaves. This will enable them to establish their roots more readily. Be sure to avoid disturbing the root ball, preferably by wrapping it in burlap. It is essential that the roots not dry out during the transplanting.

Prepare the planting hole with good loam, composted manure, and peat moss. (Hollies need an acid soil.) After planting, prune the shrubs and mulch the soil surface with leaves, compost, pine needles, or any other acid mulch that will prevent water evaporation. During dry periods water the soil faithfully and spray the shrubs themselves during the first year.

We have a holly that bears beautiful berries. A friend who planted one has no luck with hers. When she bought it she was told it was a female holly. She has read that in order for hollies to bear fruit two plants are needed—one male and one female. Why does our single holly have berries?

While it is true that most hollies bear male and female flowers on separate plants (see the full explanation in the answer to the preceding question), some of the newer varieties of holly are self-pollinating. It could also be that your holly has had a male branch grafted onto it. If you are blessed with a lot of busy bees, this single branch is sufficient to cross-pollinate a female holly shrub. Look to see if your shrub has a branch without berries.

Your friend should ascertain, first of all, whether her holly is indeed female. When the plant blooms in early summer, examine the small white or greenish flowers. If it is female the flowers grow singly each at the end of a stem. Male flowers grow in small groups on branched stems. Female plants can be helped to fruit by spraying them with fruiting hormone available at nurseries and garden centers.

It might be worthwhile to try a temporary solution: Obtain a branch from someone who has a male tree in bloom. Put the blossoming branch in a bottle of water and hang it in the female tree where the bees can get to it.

At Christmas time I was given a small variegated-leaved holly plant as a gift. It does not have any berries but I assume that is because it is too small. Can it be planted outdoors this spring? I wonder whether it will be winter-hardy in my area of southern New York State. How shall I treat it in order to make it have berries?

I strongly suspect your gift plant is probably not a holly at all. Most of the variegated-leaved "hollies" available as gift plants during the Christmas season in the Northeast are really *Osmanthus heterophyllus* (*ilicifolius*). These are actually members of the olive family. Outdoors they are fine evergreen shrubs growing up to 20 feet with yellowish green flowers followed by bluish berries, but are not winter-hardy where temperatures go below 20° F. Where you live you had best grow your osmanthus as a houseplant. Needless to say it will not grow to outdoor proportions in the house. Repot it as needed in peaty acid soil and keep it in a cool, sunny window during the winter, summering it outdoors. Feed it with an acid formula plant food.

Florists' hydrangeas make glorious flowering shrubs in large containers, or planted in the ground. Winter cold below 15° F. may kill the stems, but if well mulched the roots will send up new growth the following spring. In acid soil, the flowers will be blue; in alkaline, they will be pink. (Maynard Parker)

HYDRANGEA, FRENCH

I planted a blue French hydrangea last year, but this year the blossoms are pink. What could have caused this color change?

The flowers of French or bigleaf hydrangea (*Hydrangea macrophylla macrophylla*) are affected by the alkalinity or acidity of the soil in which it grows. In alkaline soil, which yours must be, the blossoms are pink. In acid soil the flowers are blue. If you object to having your hydrangea bear pink flowers you must change the pH of the soil in which it is growing. Try to dig in peat moss or leaf mold around the plant to which has been added cottonseed meal or aluminum sulfate. Mulch with shredded oak leaves or other acid material after the ground freezes in early winter. Conversely if you would like to keep the blossoms pink, add some lime to the soil.

My bigleaf hydrangea has a few blooms some years, however, in other years there are no blooms at all. Why is that?

Your address shows you live in southern Indiana. Bigleaf hydrangea (*Hydrangea macrophylla macrophylla*) is a more effective shrub in warmer climates. The flower buds are formed on the ends of last year's growth. In sections of the country where winter temperatures go below zero these terminal twigs are often winter killed. The years when your plants have some flowers are probably the result of milder winters.

Moving your hydrangea to a more sheltered location and wrapping it in burlap might help to mitigate some of this winter kill. Careful pruning is also an important factor in maximum bloom. These plants can be pruned only after flowering so that next year's flowering wood is not accidentally removed. Cut the old flowering shoots back to a point where vigorous growth shows and remove crowded stalks and weaker growth. Leave new shoots growing from the base.

Every flower garden needs lilacs, preferably some of today's glorious hybrids with double flowers in purest white and also in vivid purples and clear pinks. (McDonald/Mulligan)

LILACS

An ancient lilac growing on our recently purchased grounds appears to be in very bad shape. It had very few blooms last spring and is generally in a scraggly condition. Is there anything that can be done to revitalize this shrub, or should we take it out altogether?

An old lilac can be restored to vigor and full bloom by a variety of pruning methods. I don't know just how badly off your lilac is. The removal of suckers and weak or broken limbs would be the first step, plus the removal at ground level of one or two of the older stems. It might be wise, though, to allow a strong sucker to remain to grow up to replace one of the stems cut off at ground level.

137

If it has been truly neglected for many years, a combination of the pruning just mentioned plus root pruning might be in order. Dig a trench at least a foot deep and a foot wide inside the dripline of the shrub and 2 to 2½ feet from the main stems. Using pruning shears or a saw, cut off the roots you encounter, making a clean cut. (Underground cuts need not be sealed with wound paint; they will heal by themselves.)

Put a layer of several inches of rotted manure or compost in the trench. Before replacing the soil that was dug out, test it for its acid or alkaline reaction. If it tests below 6.0, add agricultural lime to balance it out. Mix more compost in the soil and refill the trench. Keep the trench moistened during dry spells for the first year.

If your lilac is truly a disaster area, remove the suckers and cut the main stems down to within one foot of the ground. You may then follow with root pruning or simply cultivate fertilizer into the soil. It will be at least three years before a lilac recovers from this radical treatment, so reserve it for a shrub you feel is severely damaged.

A lilac bush, thriving until recently, prompts me to inquire what made it stop blooming so freely. I have been told that it needs acid soil and therefore the soil acidity should be increased. But I have also been told lilacs need an alkaline soil in order to bloom. Which is correct?

Actually both opinions given you were right: Lilacs are generally very tolerant, hardy shrubs surviving a variety of conditions so long as they do have a period of winter chill. They will tolerate a slightly acid soil, though, by and large, most varieties prefer a slightly alkaline one. And they do go on for years seemingly happy though neglected. Like most growing things, however, they benefit from a little attention.

The prime factors in getting a lilac to bloom are: good sun (which also will help prevent the mildew to which these shrubs are so prone), good garden loam with a pH between 6.0 and 8.0, regular removal of basal suckers, and spent blooms which otherwise drain off energy and watering if the weather is dry while the buds are forming. As a matter of fact, trimming off the flowering heads after blooming is all the pruning these shrubs need (unless you deliberately wish to restrict normal growth). Severe pruning should only be done in the case of a shrub which is very old and deformed (see page 143). Sharp yearly pruning will remove the new wood on which the blooms appear and is one reason for lack of bloom.

Every other year spread several inches of rotted manure or compost out to the dripline of the bush and cultivate it into the soil. If the soil tests below 6.0, add an application of ground lime or woodash.

TREE PEONY

I planted a container-grown tree peony last year but have not had very good luck with it. Can you tell me why?

You don't tell me of the location of your tree peony. The flowering buds of tree peonies are developed quite early in the spring and can be damaged if they are planted in an eastern-facing site where the early morning spring sun shines on the frozen shoots injuring them. If they are in a sheltered location, by the time the sun swings south or westward, they will have had time to thaw somewhat and will be all right.

They should be planted in good loam with added moisture-retaining material, plus some sand for good drainage. The location should be away from tree roots or other invaders. The plant should be set several inches lower than it was growing in the container.

RHODODENDRON

We have a beautiful "Boule de Neige" rhododendron. It was purchased from a local nursery and we followed their planting instructions so we feel it was properly handled at

the time of planting. It bloomed nicely for the first few years, but since then has borne fewer blooms each year.

The first thing that comes to mind is to wonder whether you have been "deadheading" your rhododendron. By that I mean, after the flowers have bloomed, do you remove the old blossoms? If these are allowed to remain, the plant puts all its energy into making seeds. On the other hand, if the faded blooms are removed, the plant will then use its energy to produce more flower buds for next year's bloom.

We have some rhododendrons of the species R. *Carolinianum* **among other shrubs in a foundation planting. They are looking rather "peaked" and some of the leaves are yellowing. Although I've looked, I don't see anything on them in the way of insects that might be causing this yellowing.**

Yellowing of leaves may be caused by a number of problems. If the veins on the leaves remain green, in acid-loving plants such as rhododendron, this is most frequently caused by a lack of iron. In a foundation planting alkalinity leaches into the soil from the cement foundation and prevents the plant from absorbing iron. The yellowing of the leaves is called "chlorosis" and is a result of insufficient chlorophyl in the leaves.

First of all, I hope you are using a mulching material on the soil surrounding the rhododendrons. The feeder roots of these plants are close to the surface and may be damaged both by the intrusion of weeds and the drying out of the soil surface in dry periods. A heavy mulch of acid materials (such as oak leaves or pine needles) is valuable in counteracting both these conditions. As the mulch breaks down it also serves to keep the soil content acid. That is one way to counteract chlorosis.

The second part of the treatment is the application of an acid plant food in the early spring. Cottonseed meal, fish meal, or a liquid fish emulsion used according to the bottle directions, all are suited for these acid-loving plants. A chemical fertilizer especially devised for an acid balance may also be used, but repeated use of these may cause a

By careful selection of varieties, you can have rhododendrons like these, as well as the related azaleas, which bloom from early spring until well into the summer. They need humus-rich, moist, acid soil and shade from very hot sun. (Maynard Parker)

buildup of ammonia or aluminum in the soil, depending on the formula, both of which are toxic to plants.

If you neglected to feed these shrubs in the spring, they may be fed anytime, after blooming until the beginning of August in the Northeast, later elsewhere in the country. They are not fed any later than this so as not to stimulate young growth which will not be winter-hardy.

If you are already doing all these things and still the leaf yellowing persists, then, although you can't see them, you should not rule out the presence of spider mites. These are too tiny to be seen by the naked eye. Their presence can be detected by shaking a branch over a sheet of white paper. If rust-colored particles fall on the paper, there are the mites. Minute webs on the undersides of the leaves are also a clue to their existence. Mites can be washed off by hosing with a good forcible stream of water. Be sure to get all sides of the plant, concentrating on the undersides of the leaves. (On a hot day, get into your bathing suit and this chore will not only be fun, but you can do a good thorough job without worrying about getting wet.)

In the spring, at the time dormant spraying is done of apple trees (just as buds are swelling and temperatures are above 45 but below 85° F.) spray with a 3 percent solution of miscible oil. A rotenone preparation may be mixed with the miscible oil. Malathion also may be used as it is harmless to people, animals, and birds, but it is harmful to bees.

We bought a house which is beautifully landscaped. The eastern boundary line of our property is hedged with rhododendrons. They have had very few flowers in the three years we have owned the house, and they look rather tired.

Rhododendrons, in nature, grow in woods where they are sheltered and where there is partial shade. They should never be planted in a wind-swept eastern location in sun. Broad-leaved evergreens are dessicated by winds and the morning sun warms up the frozen buds too suddenly so that they are damaged and do not bloom.

The remedy is to either transplant them to a northern or western exposure or to erect a protective barrier each winter which will shield them from wind and sun. Drive stakes slightly taller than the rhododendrons at suitable intervals and attach burlap to them.

Keep them mulched with shredded oak leaves, or other acid material, and feed with an acid fertilizer in the spring.

ROSES

My rose bed faces south so that the bushes receive full sun. They are sheltered from winds on the north side by an evergreen juniper hedge 3 feet behind them. Although this seems an ideal location, the bushes bloom sparsely.

It would seem that your rose bushes are planted too close to the juniper hedge so that these trees are absorbing much of the fertilizer present in the soil or which you apply. Roses are heavy feeders and should not be placed closer than 6 feet to shrubs, 15 feet from trees.

You can remedy this situation by moving the rose bed (in early spring when the bushes are still dormant) or by digging a narrow trench midway between the junipers and the roses. It should be 2 feet deep. Then create a barrier to keep the juniper roots from invading the rose bed by filling the trench with a wall of bricks or a sheet of metal. Cut off the invading juniper roots, but be sure to prune back the shrubs to compensate for their root loss.

Can you tell me how to prune roses for maximum bloom?

You do not mention what kind of roses you are growing. Following are general instructions for pruning the most commonly grown modern roses:

Hybrid tea roses: Until recently it was thought severe pruning was necessary. This practice is now mostly restricted to raising a few large roses on strong stems for exhibition purposes. The more wood that is left on a rose, the more blooms there will be.

Hard pruning (the term used to indicate severe pruning) should only be done at planting time so that the plant does not have too many blooms the first year but spends its energy building a sound root system. (Some growers pinch out flower buds as they appear and do not let the plant bloom at all the first year.) At planting time, cut top growth back to about 8 inches, prune damaged or dry roots, and shorten some of the longer ones. Try to cut equal amounts from tops and roots. Always make all cuts on the canes diagonal and just above a dormant outward facing bud using very sharp pruning shears.

The following year, if there are several strong new canes cut back older ones more severely. Remove branches that cross and rub. As in pruning fruit trees, the object is to maintain an open center so sun and air can get in thus helping to keep fungal diseases in check. The remaining canes

Train everblooming climbing roses on a sunny wall or fence for fragrant flowers from June until frost. (Maynard Parker)

should be cut back one-third to one-half of their height. Roses should be cut back farther in cold climates, less in warm ones.

During the blooming season, in cutting roses for indoor arrangements or removing spent ones, do not take long stems which would reduce the amount of flowering wood on the bush. Make the diagonal cut above the first five-fingered leaflet to encourage new blooming growth which will emerge just below the cut and above the leaflet.

Grandifloras, floribundas, and polyanthas are pruned by cutting last year's growth back to the second bud below the old flowering cluster, in addition to removing dead wood. Keep spent flowers removed during the growing season, cutting as for hybrid teas. Grandifloras may have the stems cut back by a quarter or, if they are too tall, to a reasonable size.

Miniatures should only have dead growth or crossing branches pruned. Tips should be lightly trimmed.

Climbers and ramblers should be cut back to 12 inches at planting time. They bloom on the previous summer's wood. Early spring pruning should only be done to remove dead and damaged canes. After blooming those canes are cut to the crown, allowing strong new canes to grow up. If too many new ones grow up, thin these out.

Large-flowered climbers, climbing hybrid teas, and climbing floribundas should only be cut back slightly at planting time. They will not develop many new canes so old ones are not cut till they no longer produce flowers. This should be done in the fall. In the spring cut out only dead or spindly growth and prune side shoots where the blossoms will be produced. Cut these shoots to two or three buds from where the shoot joins the main cane. Maximum bloom will be produced if the canes are tied horizontally on their support. Do not train canes upright as this will result in bare lower stems.

Rose trees are pruned by cutting off bloom and only to maintain the desired shape.

Pillar and shrub roses should only be thinned out when necessary and pruned to keep to desired height.

What is the proper time of year to plant roses and what location and soil should they be given?

In general, bare-root roses are planted early in the spring and in the fall (before freezing weather) in cold parts of the country. In extremely warm summer climates it is best to plant them so that the roots have taken hold before intense summer heat arrives—mid-November to mid-February. Container-grown plants can be planted any time during the growing season.

Except where summers are very hot, full sun is ideal, but

they will thrive with a minimum of six hours. In hot sections of the country midday shade is advisable. The location should be an open one so that there is good circulation of air. Avoid planting near trees or shrubs whose roots will rob the soil of the fertilizers roses need.

Plant bare-root roses as soon as received; if you cannot, cover the roots with damp material until they can be planted. The planting hole should be dug and prepared in advance. If planting bare-root roses, carry them to the planting site in a bucket of water and leave them in the water till the last moment.

Roses need rich soil. Both clay and sandy soils should have a good deal of organic material such as peat, compost, well-rotted manure of leafmold dug in. Fertilizers should also be mixed into the planting soil. Bone meal or cotton seed meal and phosphate rock will give good results as will a balanced commercial fertilizer used according to container directions. The soil should be slightly acid with a pH around 0.6.

Prune off broken or damaged dry roots and cut back the canes on the rose until 8 to 12 inches remain. Dig each planting hole 18 inches across by 18 inches deep. Space plants 2 feet apart in cold climates, 3 feet in warm ones.

Mound up soil in the middle of the planting hole and place the rose on this mound so the roots spill over the sides of the mound and the bud union is at the level you want it. The bud union is the knobby part where the hybrid rose was grafted on a sturdy understock. Where winter temperatures go below 10° F., the bud union should be just below the soil surface. In warmer climates it should be just above the soil surface.

Fill the hole, being sure there are no air pockets under the roots. When the hole is two-thirds full, firm the soil with your feet. Fill the planting hole with water and wait until it has all drained away. Then fill the hole up the rest of the way.

Mound up a little soil around the base of the canes. If planting is done in spring, remove this soil in two or three weeks or when plants begin to leaf out. In the fall, in cold climates, 6 to 8 inches should be left on the plant until new

146

Hybrid roses of all kinds are easily cultivated in sizable pots or tubs, ideally 15- to 18-inches in diameter. Be sure to water thoroughly each time, and never allow the soil to dry out severely. They need at least a half day of direct sun. (Star Roses)

growth starts in spring. In extreme cold areas with subzero weather, when the ground freezes supplement this soil mound with a mulch of evergreen boughs or salt hay. Remove soil mound by hosing off with a forceful stream of water rather than with tools which might injure the canes.

Container-grown roses should be watered thoroughly the day before planting so that the soil ball is just moist enough to remain intact around the roots during the planting. The container is removed and the rose planted so the graft is at the right level. No pruning is necessary since the roses are pruned by the nursery when started in the container.

A word about buying roses. If there is a good nursery near you buy plants which are known to be suited to the climate in which you live. If ordering by mail, study catalogs of major growers which are sent free on request. Or write to The American Rose Society (4048 Roselea Place, Columbus, Ohio 43214) for its yearly *Guide for Buying Roses.*

I would love to grow roses but they seem to require so much attention in the way of spraying and pruning. Is it possible to grow them without any fuss?

If you want healthy, freely blooming roses, they will require some attention, but really very little more than any other well-grown perennial or shrub. Good basic gardening practices will go a long way to preventing trouble because healthy plants are better able to withstand problems. If given proper planting (see page 146) with adequate sunlight and good circulation of air, the conditions which support fungal diseases (one of the main problems of roses) are lessened. Correct pruning is a must to promote strong, healthy flowering growth. This is a once-a-year chore performed in the spring (see pages 143–145).

The Encyclopedia of Organic Gardening (Rodale Press, Emmaus, Pa.) recommends that the mulches applied the previous year be removed in the spring as they may contain disease spores which have wintered over. Then they suggest that the ground around the roses remain bare for a month so that the sun can bake the soil and kill off any other spores that may be present, after which a fresh mulch may be applied.

Roses are heavy feeders and must be fertilized to produce good growth. The first feeding should be a side dressing cultivated into the soil as soon as new growth begins and before mulching. In warm parts of the country, begin feeding in February. Well-rotted manure or compost with bone meal, cottonseed meal, and dried blood are excellent for roses. A complete chemical fertilizer can also be used. Subsequent feedings should be given after blooming and can

Sweet-olive, Osmanthus fragrans, *is not hardy outdoors where temperatures drop much below 25° F., but in colder climates it makes an excellent container shrub which can be wintered over in a bright, frost-free place. The flowers appear over a long season and their fragrance is beyond description.* (McDonald/Mulligan)

be cultivated in, which will involve removing the mulch, or a liquid feeding can be given. In colder sections of the country, cease feeding by August 1.

After fertilizing, apply the fresh mulch. Mulches not only help conserve moisture in the soil and prevent weeds from growing but keep rain from splashing onto the undersides of the leaves. Rain splashing up from the soil can spread mildew, black spot and rust. If shredded bark, wood chips, sawdust, or ground corn cobs are used as mulch, additional nitrogen must be added to compensate for the loss of ni-

in the soil caused by these mulches. Blood meal is
ıt for this purpose.

do their best and bloom most freely when well wa-
...ı general this watering should be done with a soaker
so the leaves do not get wet. But an occasional showering is
necessary (especially in hot, dry areas) to remove dust from
the leaves, prevent attacks of red spider, wash off aphids
and mildew. It should be done early in the morning to give
the plants a chance to dry off before nightfall.

During the growing season pick off diseased leaves and
remove those found on the ground and destroy them. The
commonest diseases of roses are black spot, in which leaves
turn yellow and fall off (severe defoliation can kill the bush);
mildew which appears as a gray powder on the plants;
and rust which shows in orange circles on the undersides of the leaves. One method of keeping these diseases
out of the garden is to buy resistant varieties. A dormant
oil spray used before growth starts in spring is helpful
in keeping diseases in check, as well as destroying over-
wintered insect eggs. If any of these symptoms appear on
your plants and seems to be getting out of hand, it is best to
use one of the commercial preparations designed to keep
these ills at bay according to container directions. In a small
rose garden insects can be hand-picked. Pyrethrum or rotenone sprays can be used if there is an infestation.

ROSE OF SHARON

**The flowers on my rose of Sharon seem to be much smaller
than they used to be. Why have they gotten smaller?**

Your rose of Sharon (*Hibiscus syriacus*), also known as shrub
althea, will have large flowers again after a good pruning.
While the shrub is still dormant, in winter or early spring,
cut the previous year's growth back so that there are only
two or three buds left on each shoot. During the growing
season, see that your rose of Sharon is kept well watered
during dry periods.

TAMARISK

I planted a tamarisk in my seashore garden here on Cape Cod because I was told it withstands salt spray and would flower reliably here. It has proved hardy but has grown lank and is not very floriferous. Is this the nature of the shrub?

It is hard to tell from your description which of the tamarisks you have planted in your garden. Since it was recommended for seashore planting, I would assume it is one of the two which thrive best under those conditions—either *Tamarix parviflora* or *T. ramosissima* (*pentandra*). The former blooms in May and forms its bloom on growth made the previous year so it should not be pruned until after flowering. Cut back new growth to keep it shapely, and every third year or so, cut out one of the old stems at the base.

I suspect, though, from your description of its lank growth that it is *T. ramosissima* (*pentandra*). Although this is the hardiest of the tamarisks, it requires somewhat better soil than is found at the shore, so the soil should have been enriched at planting time. It blooms in July on shoots formed that season so for best results it should be pruned in spring. Cut back last year's shoots to two or three buds. Such pruning will keep it from having bare stems and will make it bloom more profusely.

If its present shape is quite unattractive, you can start over by cutting it all off less than a foot from the ground this spring. Next spring, cut the new growth to two or three buds. Yearly pruning of this sort will make for a graceful shrub covered with flowers.

8

Trees for Giant Bouquets of Bloom

The spreading branches of even a small tree bring a sculptural quality to a garden that is a necessary component in the variety of a landscape. When that tree also puts on a breathtaking display of flowers, however short the period of bloom may be, it becomes a "must" for any garden with pretensions of beauty. Fortunately, flowering trees grow in all sizes, from the dwarf flowering fruit trees to the magnificent and fast-growing tulip tree. While southern gardens can boast of the flamboyant beauty of exotic tropical specimens, there are trees that are hardy and will bloom in even the coldest areas of the country.

As with all green growing things, but more importantly in their case since most of them are larger than other garden plants, trees are valuable not only for their beauty but for their cooling shade and for the consequent "air conditioning" they bring to the atmosphere.

Since trees are the largest plant the gardener will normally deal with, their careful placement is essential in planning a garden. Not only must the needs of the tree be met as to exposure and soil, but the needs of the tree's people and plant neighbors as well. Small flowering trees do not present a major problem as they are most often planted as single specimens on the lawn. But in planting trees of larger scale, it is vital to consider their height in relation to the house and the property and the shade they will throw. While on a hot summer day shade is one of the reasons for planting a tree, if it is too dense on neighboring shrubbery, perennials, and annual plants, those will not perform as they should.

If you are in doubt about which flowering tree you would like to have and is right for your area, try to visit local public gardens, arboretums, and plant nurseries at blooming time to help you make a choice. If you are in doubt as to the hardiness of a tree you would love to have, consult your county extension agent or a good garden encyclopedia.

BRADFORD PEAR

I planted a Bradford pear in a bowl-shaped depression back of our house because I thought it would be sheltered from winds. Some years the buds start to open quite early and are blasted by early spring cold spells. I wonder if it is getting too much warmth for its own good and whether it should be moved to a more open spot. If so, how do I go about transplanting it?

I think you have analyzed the problem with your Bradford pear (*Pyrus calleryana* "Bradford") perfectly. Obviously, on a sunny day this spot collects and reflects enough heat to start your tree into bloom ahead of time. Bradford pears are quite hardy and can withstand wind so that you could safely move it to a more exposed location without harming the tree. Following are instructions which apply to transplanting any deciduous tree. Preparations begin in the spring a year ahead of the actual move.

Technically if a tree's trunk is less than 5 inches in diameter it is considered feasible to move it. However, with a tree of such size, it would be necessary to use equipment not found in the average garden. For instance, a truck would be needed to handle the root ball. So while it may be "feasible" unless the tree is much smaller, it isn't really recommended for the home gardener.

In the early spring, while the tree is dormant, dig a trench about 3 feet from the trunk or to the dripline of the branches. The trench should be 2 or 3 feet deep and 18 inches wide. As you dig, prune off all roots that extend into this trench, except the very fine fibrous roots. The clean, sharp cuts should be made diagonally. Refill the trench with a mixture of half the soil that was removed and half well-rotted manure or compost. A mixture of peat moss or other soil-conditioning material may also be used. This trench must be kept moist during dry weather. Incidentally, this part of the procedure is called root pruning and can be used to revitalize an old shrub or tree that is not doing well.

The following spring, again while the tree is dormant, prepare a planting hole. It should be dug about one-third wider than the ball of earth around the tree and about 3 feet deep. As you dig the hole, keep the topsoil separate from the subsoil. Plan to discard the subsoil you have dug out. This means you will need to have on hand a like quantity of new top soil to replace it. Rotted manure, compost, or peat moss should be mixed with the top soil. If procuring top soil is difficult, substitute at least half the subsoil with manure, compost, or peat, mixing it well.

Put some of the best top soil in the bottom of the planting hole and trample it down firmly. Now dig the tree from its trench working carefully with a spading fork. It is essential in this operation that the delicate little feeder roots are not injured and that they not be allowed to dry out. If the tree is small enough, plan to wrap the root ball in wet burlap. Otherwise, put wet burlap or any other material which can be dampened over the roots as you uncover them. You need not be as concerned about the large downward-growing roots under the tree. Any that are difficult to excavate as you work under the tree can be cut off. This will actually benefit the tree forcing it to form new feeder roots. It is the care with which these feeder roots are treated that will insure the success of moving the tree.

To compensate for the loss of roots, the top of the tree will need to be cut back as well. Prune back about one-third of the tree's small branches and tip twigs.

Pad a wheelbarrow with straw, old blankets, or anything you have to keep the bark on the trunk from being injured. Plan this phase of the operation so you work continuously from the time the tree is lifted out of the earth, moved, set in its planting hole, and the hole filled in. Do not let the tree sit around while you stop for lunch before replanting it.

The tree should be set in the hole so that it is straight and will finish up planted at the same level it was before. Do not set it more deeply nor more shallowly. You can plan to place it so the earth around it will be below the level of the surrounding soil forming a basin which will facilitate watering it well.

If more soil needs to be filled in before the tree is at the right level, trample that down again so there are no air pockets. If you do not have enough topsoil for the entire planting, use the best soil first, reserving that mixed with subsoil for the upper part of the hole. Fill in around the tree, tamping the earth firmly under and around the roots as you go. Be sure to prune any roots that are injured during the planting process. Work carefully, packing the earth with your feet as the hole is filled in so that no air pockets are left under roots. Water the tree in well and, as the earth settles around it, add more soil as needed.

The tree should be staked to keep it from heaving out of the ground or settling crookedly. A small tree should have a stake to hold it. The stake should be driven into the ground before the tree is planted. For a larger tree, drive equidistant stakes into the ground beyond the fresh soil. Wire looped around the tree near the lowest branches should be attached firmly to the stakes. Pass the wire through cut sections of old gardening hose so that the wire is not in direct contact with the tree trunk or branches. Taut wire would injure the bark.

During the first season the tree must never be allowed to dry out. A mulch on the new soil will help conserve moisture, but water deeply whenever there is no rain. The guy wires should be left on the tree for at least two years till it has had time to rebuild its root system and hold on for itself.

CHERRY, FLOWERING

We have a Japanese flowering cherry planted as a specimen in our lawn. It does not flower as well as it should though it is healthy and the foliage is fine. We had it pruned professionally last year in an effort to make it bloom. That helped, but not much. What can we do to make it bloom?

It is hard to guess what could be wrong with your Japanese cherry (*Prunus serrulata*). They are usually quite free flowering with minimal care. One thought occurs to me. Is your lawn heavily fertilized? It may be that the high nitrogen content of the lawn fertilizer is causing your tree to overwork itself producing foliage at the cost of setting flower buds. Next time the lawn is fed, make sure you keep away from the area where the tree's roots are.

I understand flowering cherries do not bloom successfully in California. Is this true?

Many of the ornamental flowering varieties of fruit trees, including cherries, seem to need a period of winter cold to set their blooms. In the sections of southern California where there is no appreciable drop in winter temperatures, they are not at their best. One variety that does seem to successfully produce flowers in that climate is the Taiwan flowering cherry (*Prunus campanulata*).

CHESTNUT

I would like to grow an edible variety of chestnut both for the flowers and the nuts. I understand the American chestnut is almost extinct, but are other kinds available?

As you have been told, the American chestnut (*Castanea dentata*) has been to all intents and purposes wiped out since fungus destroyed it early in this century. It is to be hoped that someday a cure for the fungus will be found or a

disease-resistant variety will be developed. In the mean-
time, the most reliably disease-resistant chestnuts are of
Chinese parentage (*C. mollisima*). If only one of these trees
is planted, flower and fruit production will be scant. It is
necessary to plant two for cross-pollination. Two choice
disease-resistant varieties are "Orrin" and "Crane." Since
these grow to 50 feet, they need a fair amount of room.

CRAB, FLOWERING

**Our house is on a very small lot. I would like to plant an
ornamental flowering crab tree on our lawn. Because I am a
bird lover, I always try to use plants which will have fruit
for migrating birds and so am especially interested in the
fruit of the flowering crab. My neighbor, who has red
cedars in her yard, tells me that if I plant a flowering crab
both it and her red cedars will develop a disease called
"rust." Is this true?**

Yes, the beautiful pink-flowering American crabs are subject to the fungus called cedar-apple rust. The oriental varieties, however, are rust-resistant. One of the most beautiful
and most popular of these—the Sargent crab (*Malus sargen-
tii*)—also holds its red fruit late into the fall so that they will
be a feast for migrating birds. It is available both as a
spreading shrub or as a dwarf tree growing 6 to 8 feet, but
with a spread up to 20 feet. The Japanese flowering crab (*M.
floribunda*), is taller but still suitable for a small garden. It
grows to 20 feet with a spread to 25 feet. The flower buds
are dark pink fading to white as the blossoms open. The
small fruits are red and yellow.

DOGWOOD, FLOWERING

**We have a flowering dogwood planted in the lawn here in
southern Massachusetts which does not bloom reliably.**

157

Flowering crab apples, peaches and cherries, are among the garden's best small flowering trees for spring bloom. (Maynard Parker)

Three years ago it had few flowers. I thought it might have a disease but the following year it bloomed well. This year, though, it had few flowers again. What can I do to make it bloom more regularly?

In its native habitat, flowering dogwood (*Cornus florida*) grows among larger trees so that it is somewhat shaded and sheltered from wind and sun. If a dogwood is planted in an open situation, the spring sun warms the exposed tree and encourages the buds to start opening. An unseasonal drop in temperature or the icy blasts of a late storm cause the opening buds to be injured. If the injury is serious enough, those buds will not flower. If it is not a very large tree, you might plan to move it to a more sheltered and somewhat shaded location. Please note, however, that dogwoods do not take kindly to being transplanted, therefore only do so if it is small enough to be handled under optimum conditions.

For instructions on how to transplant your tree, see Bradford pear.

DOGWOOD, EVERGREEN

An evergreen dogwood planted in our garden in southern Louisiana three years ago has not flowered at all. What can we do to make it bloom?

Evergreen dogwood (*Cornus capitata*), a lovely Himalayan native hardy only in mild parts of the country, is a slow bloomer. I'm afraid there's nothing you can do to make it bloom, except wait. These trees do not begin to bloom until they are eight or ten years old. But it is well worth the wait as it is an especially beautiful species. The creamy flowers are followed in the fall by strawberry-shaped red fruits. The Japanese flowering dogwood (*C. kousa*) also takes some years to come into bloom, and it, too, is well worth the time it takes.

159

Although crape-myrtle is treasured for its long flowering season in the summer, it has beautiful bark in all seasons, as shown here in early spring at Colonial Williamsburg, Williamsburg, Virginia. (McDonald/Mulligan)

Flowering dogwood is available in numerous improved varieties, both with white and pink flowers. (J. Horace McFarland Company)

161

Japanese dogwood, Cornus kousa, *blooms in early summer, after the more common* Cornus florida *types have finished. Both kinds have attractive red fruit and colorful foliage in autumn.* (McDonald/Mulligan)

162

DOGWOOD, JAPANESE

I would like to plant a small tree for spring bloom. I like the dogwoods because they are such beautiful trees, but it seems to me they are in bloom for a very short period. Is there a variety that blooms for a longer time?

I suggest you try to see a specimen of the Japanese dogwood (*Cornus kousa*). It blooms later than the common flowering dogwood (*C. florida*), usually in June and July. Basically, a multistemmed shrub, it can be trained as a small tree and purchased as such from a nursery. It will ultimately reach 20 feet in height. The flowers (actually bracts surrounding the true flowers) are smaller than those of the usual eastern or western American dogwoods, but the four pointed petals are exquisitely beautiful, creamy white becoming pink at the edges as they age. The blooms appear after the leaves. In the fall the foliage is yellow and scarlet and the red fruits look like strawberries.

DOVETREE

On a recent trip to the Pacific Northwest I saw a beautiful flowering tree I had not heard of before called a dovetree. Can you tell me whether it will grow and flower here in southern Missouri?

The lovely bracts of the dovetree (*Davidia involucrata*) make this a most desirable tree for the home garden. It is said to grow to 30 feet, but in its native China it grows taller. The true flowers are not showy, but the two creamy white bracts of different size that envelope them make the tree, when in bloom, look as though it were covered by a flight of doves. The appearance of these bracts also gives rise to the tree's other common name, "Handkerchief Tree."

It may be hardy with winter protection as far north as New York City, so it will certainly be fully hardy where you live. If yours is a very hot location with drying winds in summer, plant it where it will have some shelter and partial shade. One word of caution: the dove tree will have to attain some years of maturity before it will come into bloom—ten to twenty years. One variety—considered a species by some experts—*Vilmoriniana,* is faster growing and so may bloom sooner.

EMPRESS-TREE

There is a large deciduous tree on our property in northern New Jersey with very large leaves (almost a foot long). It has recently been identified by a friend of ours from the South as an empress-tree. She says it should bear violet, foxglove-shaped flowers in the spring before the leaves appear. We have observed flower buds on the tree but it has never bloomed. What could be wrong with it?

The empress-tree (*Paulownia tomentosa*), although winter-hardy as far north as Connecticut, is at its best in the South. The flower buds are formed in the fall and remain on the tree through the winter so that they are killed by the cold and fail to bloom.

FRANKLIN TREE

I would like to plant a Franklin tree in my northern California garden. Is this a good choice?

The Franklin tree (*Franklinia alatamaha*) should grow well in your garden since it thrives under the same conditions as rhododendron. It is an especially lovely small tree, deservedly popular with its beautiful white blossoms which sometimes persist late enough to be set off by the brilliant red autumn foliage. Like rhododendron, it needs an acid, peaty soil and, in hot areas, partial shade. Otherwise it should be planted in full sun. It is shallow-rooted, so avoid cultivating around it. One word of caution, during an especially wet season it may not bloom well.

FRINGETREE

Our fringetree (although it is more shrubby than treelike) has beautiful clusters of white flowers in the spring, but there are very few blue berries.

The native American fringetree (*Chionanthus virginicus*) often bears male and female flowers on separate plants. The male flowers are showier, but the female ones produce the blue fruit. To make sure of getting a female you should obtain a container-grown plant when the fruits are present. The shrub can be induced to become treelike by removing the lowest branches over a period of time as it grows.

We bought a new home last year. We were told that the tree on the lawn was a fringetree or old man's beard. Now, well into spring, it is not leafing out and appears to be dead. What could have killed it? It is not a newly planted tree.

By now you may have discovered there is nothing wrong with your fringetree (*Chionanthus virginicus*). Fringetrees are just slow to come into leaf and bloom, sometimes waiting until summer to do so.

FRINGETREE, CHINESE

A chinese fringetree planted some seasons ago does not flower well. It is planted in a border on the western side of the house.

The Chinese fringetree (*Chionanthus retusus*), like its American relative (*C. virginicus*) needs full sun to bloom its best. These shrubby trees are easily transplanted (in early spring or fall) and you might move it to a sunnier spot for better bloom. The Chinese fringetree will also profit by having the planting hole deeply prepared and enriched with well-rotted manure or compost.

GOLDEN-CHAIN TREE

I love the yellow, wisterialike blooms of the golden-chain tree. Can you tell me if it is winter-hardy in cold climates? Any information you can give me to make it bloom well would be appreciated.

Yes, golden-chain (*Laburnum*) is winter-hardy. Most species of these trees are relatively easy to grow and blossom. In highly alkaline soil they tend to an iron deficiency called chlorosis. To counteract this, feed with an acid-formula plant food or fish meal emulsion.

Wherever possible the beanlike seed pods should be removed to prevent a drain on the tree's energy resulting in poorer blooming the following year. One of the best varieties to look for is *L.* x *watereri* Vossii.

If you have small children, I would not recommend planting this tree as the pods and all parts of the tree are poisonous.

GOLDEN-RAIN TREE

We are looking for a shade tree which would also bloom and be relatively trouble free. I love the golden-rain tree, but wonder whether it would withstand drought during our hot, dry Kansas summers.

The golden-rain tree (*Koelreuteria paniculata*) is an especially rewarding tree which seems to meet all your qualifications. It is a well-shaped tree (prune it to shape when it is young)

166

of medium size forming a round head, with feathery leaves and long yellow flower clusters. The latter are followed by three-sided papery fruits which resemble Chinese lanterns.

It needs full sun, tolerates alkaline soil and drought. (It will need to be watered during dry periods while it is young.) In areas of high winds it should be planted where there is some protection as it may be topheavy when in bloom.

GOLDEN-SHOWER TREE

While on a trip to Hawaii I saw the most spectacular flowering tree called a golden-shower. Would it grow back home here in Beverly Hills, California?

The golden-shower tree (*Cassia fistula*), also called shower of gold is one of the native Indian senna trees. It is one of the least hardy of the sennas. You might be successful with it, but some years it might not bloom. It is marginal in your area. A more reliable bloomer where you are, and nearly as spectacular, is the gold-medallion tree (*C. leptophylla*). There are also a number of shrubby varieties which would flower well in your garden.

HAWTHORN

Our English hawthorn "double pink" has exquisite blooms but very few "haws" in the fall. How can we get it to fruit more prolifically?

I'm afraid there is nothing to be done. The double varieties of English hawthorn (*Crataegus laevigata [oxyacantha]*) do not fruit as well as single varieties. The same is true of some Canadian hybrids. You could, if you have room, plant another variety for a fall display of fruits, such as *C. o.*

167

"Gireoudii" which has large red fruits. C. x *lavallei* has large orange-red fruit and the leaves turn bronze-red in the fall. The Washington hawthorn (C. *phaenopyrum*), which is larger than most, has orange and bright red fall color and red fruits which last well into winter.

The leaves on a branch of our hawthorn tree have turned brown and the branch appears to be dying. What is wrong with it?

It sounds like a case of fire blight. Withered leaves and shriveled, blackened shoots (looking as though they've been scorched by fire) during the growing season are the symptoms of this bacterial disease. It seems to prevail in very wet seasons. Prune the branch off and burn it and any leaves that may have fallen. Disinfect the pruning tools. Spray with weak Bordeaux mixture or a streptomycin spray. If you cannot find the streptomycin spray consult the Agricultural Experimentation Station in your locality.

While examining some yellow spots on the leaves of my hawthorn tree, I turned up the leaves to discover little bumps on the undersides. Can you tell me what these are?

This is a disease called juniper apple rust. I would venture to guess that somewhere in the vicinity of your hawthorn there is a red cedar growing. Hawthorns, which like apples are members of the Rose Family, are both alternate hosts for this disease which initiates its cycle on the cedar and completes it on the member of the Rose Family.

Rainy, cool weather favors the development of rust and it is spread by wind and raindrops. To reduce the incidence of rust, clean up all fallen and diseased leaves. (Do not compost them.) Examine junipers for the galls which contain the spores—sometimes called cedar apples—and remove and burn them. If the red cedar is on your property and is not a cherished tree, cutting it down would end your problems. Asiatic species of hawthorn are less susceptible to juniper apple rust than the American ones.

JACARANDA

We have a jacaranda tree which does not flower. Our home is just north of San Francisco in the Bay area. How can we get our jacaranda to flower?

I'm afraid the problem is beyond your control. Jacaranda trees need intense summer heat to flower and winter temperatures that do not drop below 25° F. Their flowering is also inhibited by ocean winds. Southern California and Florida seem to be the most reliable areas for jacarandas.

MAGNOLIA

We wish to plant a Yulan magnolia where we live just outside of Phoenix, Arizona. Can you tell us how to plant and maintain it for the best bloom?

Yulan magnolia (*Magnolia heptapeta* [*denudata*]) should be an excellent tree for your climate, providing you have the room for a good-size spreading tree. (It grows 35 to 50 feet with a spread of 30 feet.) It will be six to seven years before it comes into bloom. Like most magnolias it will require a rich, slightly humusy soil. Have your soil tested as heavily alkaline soil does not suit magnolias.

Be sure your specimen is balled and burlapped when you buy it. The fleshy roots of magnolia can easily be damaged during planting. (One reason why native ones are difficult to dig in the wild.) If the roots are protected by a ball of earth, you will have no problem.

Keep the ultimate size of the tree in mind when planting it so that years hence you do not have trouble with the branches crowding into the house or other trees. Magnolias do not take kindly to pruning, and removing large branches could eventually lead to the loss of the tree. Only small twiggy growth can safely be cut—allowing you to bring some of the large, white, fragrant blossoms indoors for enjoyment. Of course, you will have no choice if a branch is injured during a storm. In that event, prune it so the cut is clean and carefully seal it with wound paint.

My husband and I recently retired. We would very much like to plant a magnolia tree in our small new garden, but have been told that it may take twenty years before one comes into bloom—rather too long for us to wait. Can you recommend one that might bloom sooner, would not be too large, and would be hardy here in southern Pennsylvania?

Saucer magnolia is one of the most beautiful of the small flowering trees; it blooms in early spring. (McDonald/Mulligan)

It is true that many of the magnificent magnolia specimens may need to be ten to twenty years old before they are ready to bloom. But there are winter-hardy small ones that bloom much earlier. The Kobus Magnolia (*Magnolia kobus*), which takes fifteen years to come into bloom, has many hybrids and varieties that bloom in as little as three years. This may account for the popularity of one of these—the star magnolia (*M. stellata*)—which tends to be shrubby, rather than treelike, and blooms in three years. The variety *M. s.* "Rosea," the pink star magnolia, blooms pink.

Both of these bloom so early that the flowers can be nipped by frosts. If your region is subject to erratic late-spring frost, plant it in a sheltered northern exposure where the buds will be slow to open and so will not be damaged by frost. *M. s.* "Waterlily" has broader petals than the two already mentioned and is supposed to be more vigorous and faster growing. The varieties of saucer magnolia (*M. soulangiana*) are tree-like, growing to 25 feet, but are also winter-hardy and have larger flowers, about 6 inches in diameter. They bloom in a range of shades from white to pink to purple-red. To make sure of the color you are getting, buy a named variety.

M. s. "Liliputan" is somewhat smaller than the others and its pink and white blooms are also smaller, but is later blooming so it will not be injured by frosts.

Another good species is *M. salicifolia* which is a slow-growing tree, tall and narrow in shape, with willowlike foliage and white star-shaped flowers. Called the anise magnolia, the species may take ten years to bloom, but the variety "W. B. Clarke" blooms when it is younger.

REDBUD, WESTERN

Last spring, at the invitation of a friend who has some property in the foothills of the Sierras, I dug up a native western redbud and moved it to my home in southern California. It does not flower as lavishly as the ones that grow on my friend's land.

I would guess that the problem is that you live in an area that is a little warmer than is appreciated by your western redbud. The flowers seem to do best on trees planted where the winter temperatures go below 25° F.

SILK TREE

Will a silk tree grow if planted here in Tennessee or is this too far north for the southern "mimosa."

The more usually grown silk tree (*Albizia julibrissin*) might have trouble growing as far north as Tennessee, but the variety called the pink silk tree (*A. j.* "Rosea," or "Ernest Wilson") is said to be hardier and should be reliable where you are.

SOURWOOD TREE

A sourwood planted in our lawn is not doing well. It is a good tree for this climate (we live in Virginia), and there are others flowering nearby. Why doesn't ours?

Your climate is right for sourwood, or sorrel-tree (*Oxydendrum arboreum*), but since it needs a rather acid soil, the fact that you are growing it in your lawn makes me think that the soil may be too alkaline for it. Lawn grasses usually are limed. To remove the grass at this time would probably further damage the tree as cultivating in the vicinity of the roots is not to their liking. The best thing to do would be to apply an acid fertilizer such as cottonseed meal or one prepared for rhododendrons. Then mulch with shredded oak leaves or other organic mulch that will break down and add acidity to the soil. Conditions suited to rhododendrons (acid soil and moisture) are exactly what these trees need.

TULIP-TREE

How can I get a tulip-tree to bloom? Mine is about 25 feet high and has not yet bloomed.

Tulip-trees, both *Liriodendrom tulipifera*, the American species, and *L. chinense* from China, are most commonly grown from seed. As a result they are slow to bloom. Yours is still a baby since these trees may attain a height of 200 feet. I think patience is the solution to your problem. At the time of planting—spring is the most desirable time of year, incidentally—I hope that it was in deep, rich loam in a cool moist location. If these conditions were not provided, there is not much you can do now because these trees do not transplant well. You might mulch it with compost or rotted manure each spring and keep it well watered during dry periods.

YELLOW-WOOD

Our beautiful yellow-wood tree does not bloom reliably. What can the trouble be?

Yellow-wood (*Cladrastis lutea*) does not bloom reliably every year, usually alternating one year of good bloom with one scant one. It is the nature of the tree, but its creamy white fragrant flowers are worth waiting for. If the tree is still a young one, pinching off some of the flowering shoots so that it does not bear too many blossoms while the tree is young may help to improve its bloom when it is older.

9

House Plants that Really Bloom

The darlings of the green-growing world are the house plants. In recent years I have not visited a home or apartment—no matter how small and humble, or elegant and opulent—that did not have a plant or two. More often there are far more than two, and it is evident that the home owner is a victim of plantomania. Indeed some homes are so burgeoning with plants (my own included) that the logistics of placing them and still having room for furniture are a major problem.

I once had a house guest suggest that my home would be more efficiently run if I did not have so many plants to care for. The suggestion that I dispose of them was almost as shocking as it would have been had she suggested I dispose of my children.

If you're a victim of the disease, you know it well. Your first plant does not succeed and you say, "I guess I don't have a green thumb." But another day a flowering beauty catches your eye in a plant shop window (or even at the supermarket), or someone gives you one for your birthday, and you try again. Eventually success (or stubbornness in refusing to admit defeat) crowns your efforts.

You learn to take cuttings and start your own plants, and the number of pots grows. A trade with a friend of one of your self-started specimens brings a new kind into the house and . . . you have fallen victim to the disease. Personally, I admire people who can limit their plant population to two or three exquisitely grown specimen plants positioned for their architectural and decorative value, but I am of a different breed.

Flowering plants are somewhat more of a problem to grow in the average home than green foliage plants. Sunlight is in many cases more of a prerequisite than it is with green plants. But lack of sun needn't be a deterrent as it can be artificially provided by growing the plants under lights. Planned light gardens make an attractive feature to brighten any dark corner.

AFRICAN VIOLET

Why is it that whenever I buy an African violet covered with blossoms, once they fade it never again blooms so profusely again or very often?

Several things are necessary to produce a good crop of blooms on an African violet plant. The most important is light. East or west windows are considered perfect for violets—but other factors should be taken into consideration. When I lived in New York City with its smog and tall buildings throwing shadows for portions of the day, I found my violets did best in south-facing windows except during July and August. Now that I live in an outer suburb, I keep most of my violets in an eastern window. I have luck, though, with some that are in a north-facing window because, since we are on a hillside, the lawn on the northern side of the houses rises bowl-shaped and reflects quite a bit of sunlight into the north windows. (When there is snow on the lawn, the reflection is intense.)

Flourescent lights are, of course, tailor-made for African violet needs. Give the plants at least fourteen hours of fluorescent lights a day and adjust the distance according to the size of the plant. The tops of the plants should be about 10 inches from the lights. Both under lights or in natural

Of all the flowering house plants, the African violet, shown here in a small-growing, double-flowered type, is perhaps the easiest to coax into almost nonstop bloom. Give it bright light or some direct sun (especially in the winter), or grow in a fluorescent-light garden; keep the soil evenly moist with water of room temperature. (McDonald/Mulligan)

light you will know by the growth pattern if your plant's light needs are being met: If the stems reach upward, they are not getting enough; if the stems curls down over the pot rim, they are getting too much.

Water with warm water whenever the soil surface begins to feel dry to the touch. Water may be applied from above or from the bottom, but never, never let the pots sit in water for any length of time. Water more freely as they are coming into bloom and while blooming; then when the flowers fade, let them rest a little by going a little dryer between waterings.

Humidity is another important factor in African violet bloom. When I first became interested in house plants many years ago, I had a lone violet sitting on a window sill. It carried on bravely for years but never bloomed. When the craze really hit me and my husband installed glass shelves across a pair of windows to house my overflow collection, they all did well. I think a collection of plants provides itself with a certain amount of humidity.

A better way to make sure there is adequate moisture in the air around your violets is to set them over trays of pebbles filled with water. The plants should be in saucers so the pots don't stand in water. Misting is not recommended as it can spot the leaves. Running a humidifier in your home is best of all because it will benefit the humans in the house as well. We can use the humidity, too.

Any of the prepared African violet soil mixes on the market or the newer soilless mixes are fine for violets. With the latter you will need to fertilize with each watering since there is no organic content in these mixes. Use the fertilizer in a more dilute amount than recommended. If you make up your own soil for violets, two things are important: it must be sterile and should be light enough to allow delicate African violet roots to penetrate it. (You can sterilize soil by baking it in the oven at 200° F. for three hours.)

Use fish emulsion or any commercial African violet plant food with an analysis such as 5-10-5. Avoid foods that are higher in nitrogen (the first number) than in phosphorus (the second number). The soil must be damp before fertilizer is applied or it will burn the roots. A good practice is to feed the day after watering. (That is why a dilute solution should be used with the soilless mix.)

Normal house temperatures are agreeable to these plants, which is probably one reason why they are such popular house plants. Temperatures below 55° F. at night are definitely detrimental to their setting blooms. Really cold conditions will cause the plants to die. If your violets are on the window sill, move them back from the glass during freezing weather or protect them by inserting folded newspapers between them and the glass to cut down drafts.

You may find, as I have, that despite meeting all the conditions described above, some plants will bloom more freely while some just will not bloom as often. The reason for this seems to be that some varieties are just more florifer-

To grow African violets and other flowering plants in a fluorescent-light garden, provide a minimum of two 20-watt tubes in a reflector, as shown here. Burn the lights 12-to-16 hours out of every 24. (Mc-Donald/Mulligan)

ous than others. When I find a variety that is a prolific bloomer, I make a point of starting two or three new plants at regular intervals. This assures me that, should some disaster strike my original plant, I will not lose this satisfactory variety. And I nearly always have a specimen at peak bloom to give as a gift.

New plants are easily started from a single leaf. Take a middle-size leaf—not a large one from the outer row of leaves, nor a small one from the center. The stem of the leaf should be cut to about 1 or 1½ inches in length. Make the cut diagonally across the stem. Let it sit for several hours to callous, then dust it with rooting hormone. It can be rooted in water, but I find these roots are rather weak and as new plantlets form, it is hard to keep from drowning them. I prefer sand as a rooting medium, although vermiculite, a mixture of sand and peat moss, or a soilless mix will all do well. Use a 1½- to 2-inch plastic pot and invert a glass of suitable size over it to form a miniature greenhouse. Tilt the glass from time to time to allow excess moisture to evaporate and allow some circulation of air. Or seal the whole pot in a baggie and make a few slits in the baggie. Set the leaf in a warm spot where there is bright light but no midday sun.

Never allow the soil to dry out while roots are forming. Eventually plantlets will form. At this time, water occasionally with very diluted plant food. When these are something over an inch in height, separate them and plant them in individual pots in a very light soil.

AZALEA

Can I keep a gift azalea indoors as a house plant?

Azaleas can be kept from year to year as house plants providing you can give them a relatively cool, sunny place with freshly moving air. During the winter indoors they will take more sun than their outdoor relatives and an east, south, or west windowsill will suit them. An unheated enclosed porch is ideal. An overheated house or apartment with daytime temperatures constantly over 70° F. will dry them up.

Like their outdoor counterparts, they need an acid soil, which should be kept evenly moist, and they should be regularly fed with an acid formula plant food.

After blooming they can be pruned to shape to keep them at a size suitable for indoor culture. Repot them at this time, if necessary, prying the old soil out gently from among the roots. Use an acid-type soil such as for African violets with some additional sand. Mist them at least twice a day when new roots are forming. As soon as the weather has warmed up, if at all possible, set them outside in partial shade. The soil may be allowed to go almost dry at this time, but never let a potted azalea dry out entirely. Bring it back indoors with the other houseplants in early fall. Do not fertilize it while buds are forming. Mist regularly.

The buds on my tender indoor azalea turned brown and fell off without opening this spring. What would have caused this?

Azaleas thrive and bloom best in a cool, humid atmosphere (see page 179). Obviously you must have provided these conditions in your house or the azalea would not have set buds in the first place. Perhaps after the buds formed your plant was moved into a place where it received too much sun, or the humidity was allowed to drop, or the temperature in your house was turned up. It is possible too, that the soil was kept too soggy after the plants came into bloom. The soil for potted azaleas needs to be kept evenly moist but not sopping wet.

BEGONIA

I have a hanging basket begonia of the Cleopatra variety. Although it is very lavish, it never produces bloom. I am careful to keep it moist but not soggy at all times. Why does it not bloom?

A little well-planned neglect might help your begonia to bloom. Rhizomatous begonias bloom best when they are allowed to dry out a little between waterings—naturally not to the point of wilting. But the soil surface should feel dry to the touch before watering.

I wonder if you may have been feeding it with a plant food high in nitrogen. Nitrogen induces strong foliar growth. Phosphorous encourages blooming. Use a plant food such as for African violets, with an analysis of 5-10-5 to promote blooms.

To keep the roots from being waterlogged, the soil should be a light one. A prepared soilless mix is excellent (especially for a hanging basket as these mixes are lightweight), only then you must use a dilute fertilizer at every watering. In prepared potting soil, at least one-fourth of the mix should be perlite or vermiculite.

Hybrid "angel-wing" begonias bloom over a long season and may be displayed on a pedestal or grown in a hanging basket. (McDonald/Mulligan)

BEGONIAS, RIEGER

I cannot seem to be successful with the beautiful Rieger begonias. Can you tell me how to keep one of these plants going?

The Rieger begonias should be an ideal house plant as they tolerate average house temperatures and they seem to be

Rex begonias flower, but they are grown mostly for the richly-colored and variegated leaves. (McDonald/Mulligan)

one of the few plants that do not need a lot of humidity to thrive. As a matter of fact, I gave my first one a bad case of mildew by misting it religiously. Soggy soil is sure to induce rotting of the stems. Water only when the soil surface begins to go dry. These plants are also sensitive to overfeeding. Use an African violet house plant fertilizer at half the strength recommended.

Leaf and stem cuttings of begonias, African violets and most other house plants will root quickly in a glass-enclosed case like this one (it was once used as an aquarium), placed in bright natural light, or under two 20-watt fluorescent tubes as shown here. (McDonald/Mulligan)

As with all begonias, the soil mix in which it is planted should be rather light—add extra vermiculite or perlite to potting soil, and do not pack the mixture around the roots. To bloom these plants need good light—an east or west window year round or a south-facing one in winter.

BELLFLOWER, ITALIAN

I have repeatedly tried to grow Italian bellflower (star of Bethlehem) as a hanging basket plant. It is fine on our shady patio all summer, but soon after it is brought into the house it loses its blooms and dries up. Does it just not grow in the house?

Italian bellflower (*Campanula isophylla*) is not easy to winter over if your house is of average temperature. If you have a cool room or enclosed, unheated sun porch where it can be kept in good light but not in direct sun, then you should be successful. When you bring your bellflower in, cut it back a few inches and reduce waterings so that it goes dry between waterings. Withhold fertilizer altogether. In the spring, move it where it will get a little morning sunlight and increase watering, keeping it evenly moist. Resume feeding with a high phosphorous plant food. Put it back outdoors as soon as danger of frost is past.

BIRD-OF-PARADISE

My five-year-old bird-of-paradise has yet to bloom. Does it just not bloom as a house plant?

Queen's bird-of-paradise (*Strelizia reginae*) is grown most successfully as a greenhouse plant, but can be induced to bloom in the house. The principal reason yours is not blooming is because it is still too young. These plants must be from six to twelve years old before they bloom.

Bird-of-paradise should be repotted in autumn or early spring in two parts good loam, one part peat, and some added sand for good drainage. But because these plants need to be fairly pot-bound to come into bloom, cease repotting when a 9-inch pot is reached.

It should have full sun, or as much as you can manage. Keep it rather dry during the winter until new growth begins. When you increase watering, feed it with a fertilizer low in nitrogen, such as one for African violets. It needs good humidity and daytime winter temperatures should not exceed 70° F. Night-time temperatures should not drop below 50° F. Summer it outdoors with light shade at midday.

In southern California and Florida these plants are grown out of doors where they bloom intermittently all year. The clumps should not be divided frequently since they produce more blooms when their roots are crowded.

Amaryllis grow from bulbs planted indoors in the fall for flowers in the winter. (McDonald/Mulligan)

BROMELIADS

I would very much like to grow bromeliads but have been told they are difficult under ordinary house conditions. Do they flower reliably?

Many bromeliads are available these days and will grow well in the average home. Most will not thrive if grown in hot, stale, dry air. They like a good deal of humidity and fresh, moving air. If you do not have a humidifier on your furnace, it would be a good idea to have a portable humidifier. Otherwise, hand-misting the leaves is a must. (The additional humidity is good for people, too.) They also need to always have the central cups formed by the leaves supplied with water.

For the general care of bromeliads, see Queen's tears,

pages 204–206. *Billbergias,* such as Queen's tears, are one of the easiest to grow in a home. But there are many others available from mail-order houses and some to be found in florists' and plant shops. Following are some of the ones most easily found:

Aechmea, of which *A. fasciata* varieties *purpurea* and "Silver King" bloom in summer.

Ananas comosus, best known of the bromeliads since it is the pineapple. You can grow your own by slicing the top off

Bromeliads like this variegated aechmea *are among the showiest and longest-lasting flowering house plants. Proper growth and bloom depends on receiving some direct sun in combination with warmth and high humidity. (McDonald/Mulligan)*

Shower bromeliad leaves with tepid water twice a week; fill the cup in the center with fresh water; drench the growing medium with tepid water at the same time, but do not leave the pot standing in a saucer of water for more than a few minutes. (McDonald/Mulligan)

a pineapple and rooting it in sand after allowing the pulpy portion to dry out for a couple of days. It can be potted, after it is rooted, in soil with added vermiculite, sand, and charcoal chips. It needs sun and a lot of humidity but probably won't bear fruit as a house plant. The miniature variety sold as a house plant bears fruit more reliably.

Cryptanthus, a kind which is smaller and lower growing than most bromeliads, although the flowers are insignificant compared to the others.

Neoregelia, of which the species *N. marmorata* is called the fingernail plant because of the bright red tip on each leaf end.

Nidularium innocentii, a desirable one in which a smaller rosette of red leaves nestle among the larger olive green leaves.

Vriesia carinata which flowers in winter.

Tillandsia of which Spanish moss (*T. usneoides*) is the most unusual member.

After flowering, bromeliads like the aechmea send up offshoots, or "pups," which should be removed by cutting between the two, as shown. (McDonald/Mulligan)

Pot up the bromeliad offset as shown here. It will mature and bloom within 12-to-18 months. (McDonald/Mulligan)

CAMELLIAS—INDOORS

I yearn to grow camellias, but the climate here in Massachusetts is too severe for outdoor plants. As a compromise I have a pot-grown camellia purchased this spring. It summered outdoors in the partial shade of a tree. I have been told that since I do not have a greenhouse, it is unlikely I will be successful in getting the plant to bloom.

Many people have some success with indoor camellia culture. If you have an unheated sunporch, you will have no trouble getting your camellia to bloom—as long as you attend to its other cultural needs: for one, careful watering as too much or too little will inhibit blooming. Be sure as your camellia grows that you pot it in a slightly acid soil—good loam or compost, peat moss with some added sand, plus bone meal. Some growers recommend wood shavings be added to the soil. Begin using a plant food such as one recommended for African violets about the middle of March and use it monthly until August. Be sure soil is moist before using plant food. Summer outdoors as you have before.

Some of the newer varieties of *Camellia japonica* seem to be easier to bring into bloom under house conditions. They may not bloom as profusely as they would under ideal circumstances, but the buds they set do bloom in the house. My double-flowering camellia winters in a sunny bedroom which is cool as ordinary house temperatures go, but is nothing like the 45° F. recommended for these plants. It is close to the window glass so the temperatures may be somewhat lower than it is in the bedroom itself where night temperature readings do not go below 60.

CHRISTMAS CACTUS

I had heard that Christmas cactus will not bloom if it receives any artificial light in the fall. In September I put my Christmas cactus on a windowsill in an unused guest bedroom so that I was able to keep it out of artificial light. To my joy, it did set buds but they fall off without opening. I never brought it out into artificial light and am at a loss as to why it did not flower.

The information you had about Christmas cactus was correct, as your success in producing buds proves. The reason for withholding additional light is that (along with chrysanthemums and poinsettias) Christmas cactuses are what are called short day plants and, in nature, set their buds as the fall days get shorter. In order to flower these plants in cultivation we have to duplicate their needs. They should during this time be watered sparingly and given no fertilizer. Perhaps because your plant was in an unused room you unwittingly gave it these prerequisites enabling the plant to form flowers. However, once the buds have been formed, watering should be increased and the soil should be kept evenly moist. Either too much or too little water at this time will cause the buds to drop.

Next time the flowers have begun to open, bring your cactus out to your living area so you can enjoy the exquisite flowers.

CYCLAMEN

Last year I was given a cyclamen as a Christmas gift. Although it is alive, it has not bloomed again. How can I get it to bloom?

The beautiful cyclamens so popular as gift plants during early winter grow from a tuber. They are tender varieties (*C. persicum*) of the hardy outdoor cyclamen (*C. hederifolium* [*neapolitanum*]). In order to assure blooms a second winter, reduce the amount of water given the plants after the flowers fade.

Ideally they should be summered outdoors in as cool a spot as possible and out of direct sun. Pull off the old flowers and leaves when they come off readily. Again, they should be watered sparingly. Before bringing the plant into the house in the fall, repot the tuber in a larger pot without disturbing the rootball. Use a good house plant soil. Set the pot in a cool spot with no direct sunlight. In about a month, begin to feed with a plant food high in phosphorus (5-10-5 for instance). When growth starts it can be moved to where it gets some sunlight, but not bright midday sun. The cyclamen should bloom once more in December.

Cacti, like this collection of rebutias and mammillarias, need full sun in the spring and summer in order to bloom. It is acceptable to give them less light indoors in the winter, but temperatures should be on the cool side (50–60° F.), and the soil should be kept only barely moist. (McDonald/Mulligan)

The episcia, or flame violet, is a relative of the African violet and gloxinia. Bright, diffused sunlight, warmth and high humidity encourages flowering. (McDonald/Mulligan)

FLAME VIOLET

My flame violet has grown very lavishly but it does not seem to bloom. What do these plants require to bloom?

In order to bloom satisfactorily flame violets (*Episcia cupreata*) needs a good deal of humidity but at the same time requires warm, freshly moving air. Like African violets, they are gesneriads.

Obviously they are ideal for a warm greenhouse, but Elvin McDonald says he has seen them growing successfully in a terrarium where the covering is removed for half the day. Light should be the same as for African violets—east-west windows are best. They do very well under fluorescent light culture.

The soil in which they are potted should be a loose porous mixture supplied with both moisture retaining materials and good drawing. They also do well in soilless growing mediums providing adequate feeding is done.

FUCHSIA

I kept my lovely hanging basket fuschia on a cool porch this winter and it kept growing nicely. I repotted it in the spring into a larger basket. This summer, although I put it out on a shaded patio where it had bloomed so well last year, it did not bloom at all. What could have happened?

Fuschias need a period of dormancy in order to bloom their best. Your fuschia just didn't get its nursery winter rest. Also putting it into a much bigger pot may have been an added factor in its poor performance. Like so many other flowering plants, fuschias need to be slightly pot-bound to put on their best display.

We had some choice varieties of fuchsias growing on our shaded porch in Maine this summer. I brought them in when the weather got cold but they lost all their leaves and died.

Most varieties of fuchsias, especially the fancier hybrids, go dormant in the cold weather. You plants didn't die—at least, not at first. The recommended winter treatment for fuchsias in cold climates is to store them in good light, out of the sun, at low temperature (40 to 50° F.) and water them just enough to keep them from drying out. There seems to be two schools of thought about pruning—some experts believe they should be pruned to remove leaves and twiggy growth at the time they are brought in, others prune when new growth begins in late winter. In either case, in January they should be moved to a slightly warmer spot (but not above 65° F.) and watered more freely. If they were pruned before, check for additional dead wood and prune to shape when new growth begins. If they were not pruned earlier, cut back by half as new growth begins.

Repot them in all-purpose potting soil with added peat. When new growth is well established, begin monthly feedings which should be continued all summer. Pinch tips out to promote bushiness. As soon as the weather is reliably frost-free, put your plants back on your porch. Be sure to keep the soil evenly moist throughout the growing season.

GARDENIAS

During a recent illness of mine, a friend gave me a beautiful gardenia plant. Some of the flowers were in bloom and there were a lot of buds. As the flowers faded, the buds dropped off without opening. I have looked up gardenia in my plant book and it says it needs greenhouse culture. Should I discard my plant?

Not necessarily. It depends on what your living conditions are. Gardenias grown as houseplants need sun, daytime temperatures around 70° F., nighttime temperatures in the 60s, high humidity, and somewhat acid soil. During most of the year the plants should be kept evenly moist and they should be fed with an acid formula plant food.

In winter, watering should be lighter but gardenias must never be allowed to go dry. If it can possibly be arranged, gardenia plants should be summered outdoors in a spot where they are protected from wind and midday sun.

Clivia is an evergreen bulbous plant that sends up clusters of apricot or orange flowers once a year. (McDonald/Mulligan)

In order for clivia to bloom, it needs to be rootbound in the pot, as this one is. (McDonald/Mulligan)

When we lived in New York City in an apartment, I did keep a gardenia growing and developing an occasional flower. Now that we have our own house where we can control temperature and humidity, gardenias bloom satisfactorily. Then, as now, I kept the gardenia close to a sunny window and misted it twice a day on sunny days. I also run a humidifier.

I have had a lovely gardenia plant for ten years. Lately the flowers seem to be of smaller size and it seems to have many fewer leaves so that it looks stalky. Is it just too old to keep?

Old age does seem to be the problem with your plant. But, like you, I have an old gardenia to which I am attached. You can give it an added lease on life by pruning it to shorten some of the older leggy branches. Ideally this should be done in February. Then lift it out of its pot and prune some of the roots. You might be able to very neatly slice off about an inch of the lower roots with a sharp knife. Try to balance the amount of top and root pruning.

Repot in mildly acid soil; add peat, sand, and a little crushed charcoal to a sterilized potting soil. Mist frequently while it is reestablishing itself. Pinch off the buds it forms in the summer and resume feeding with an acid formula plant food. The buds it sets in the fall should then make somewhat larger blooms.

As a bonus, be sure to make new plants from the pruned-off parts. Any pieces of soft new wood 3 to 6 inches in length will make new plants. Insert these in sand, or sand and peat. They need to be in a warm, moist environment and to never be allowed to dry out. A propagating case with bottom heat is a professional aid to rooting cuttings, but it is possible to improvise: a terrarium set near heat, a large glass or jar inverted over each cutting, or tightly closed plastic bags are some of the methods an amateur can use. Whatever technique you use, be sure to give the cuttings a little air for about an hour each day. They should be in bright light without direct sun.

When the cuttings are rooted, pot each in a 3-inch pot

using a rich sandy loam. Return the potted plants to a shaded environment for a few days to allow the roots to take hold. Gradually expose them to more sun. If possible, set them outside for the summer. Pinch out the growing tips to make the plants bushy. Repot them into larger pots as needed and grow as recommended for gardenias on pages 194 and 196.

GERANIUM

Each fall I take cuttings from my bedding geraniums and root them and pot them up, but I never get any blossoms in winter.

Cuttings rooted in October as a rule are ready to bloom in May. It is best to think of fall cuttings as stock for next year's outdoor garden. For winter bloom indoors, take cuttings in May from your fall-rooted plants. They should be ready for indoor display the following winter.

Cuttings should be 4 or 5 inches long. Remove all but the topmost leaves. Pot them directly in a rather lean, sandy soil and keep them evenly moist while they are rooting.

Each year I try to salvage a couple of geranium plants from those on the terrace. I repot them with care in a good houseplant soil and feed them regularly. They grow lush with leaves but never bloom.

Planting geraniums in rich soil and overfertilizing them leads to good vegetative growth, which is what you are getting. Geraniums need a rather lean soil and should not be fertilized more than once a month. Use a plant food low in nitrogen and high in phosphorus (such as a 5-10-5 formula). Elvin McDonald tells of having great luck with a geranium that was potted in Jiffy Mix which has no organic content, so perhaps that is the solution. Garden soil with sand added is also good.

In the winter, these plants need as much sun as possible.

If you can put them in a cool, south-facing window that is ideal. Let them go fairly dry between waterings, then water them well. In the spring they should be given more water. As with many other flowering plants, they bloom best when a little pot-bound.

I make geranium cuttings in May for indoor bloom in winter. They are kept in a southern exposure, I feed them regularly, and their foliage is lavish but they never bloom.

Two things may be affecting your geraniums and keeping them from flowering: You may be overfeeding them with a fertilizer high in nitrogen. This results in abundant foliage growth so that all the plants' energies are expended on the leaves. Only feed them once a month, using a plant food high in phosphorous. (See the section on fertilizers in the chapter on basic gardening.) You may also be overwatering the plants. Geraniums are one of the plants in which the soil surface should be allowed to grow dry between waterings.

GLOXINIA

Some gloxinia tubers planted in individual pots have grown nicely but do not have many buds. Would repotting encourage better bloom?

You do not say what potting soil you used for your gloxinias (*Sinningia speciosa*) nor the conditions under which you are growing them. To answer your question, you might begin by repotting them. These plants require a rich soil with nutrients in the potting mix, sun, high humidity, warm temperatures (lower at night—62 to 65° F. is considered ideal), and thorough watering when the soil surface feels dry to the touch. Too low temperatures, insufficient light, inadequate humidity, too much or too little water, and too lean a soil mix are all causes of poor flowering in gloxinias.

Miniature gloxinias like these Mini-Sins require little space and bloom almost nonstop in the same conditions provided for African violets. (George W. Park Seed Co., Inc.)

Hybrid gloxinias grow from tubers that can be planted in almost any season for blooms in approximately three-to-five months. (Antonelli Brothers)

HIBISCUS, CHINESE

Must one have a greenhouse to be successful with Chinese hibiscus?

A greenhouse is almost a necessity for growing Chinese hibiscus, also Rose-of-China (*Hibiscus rosa-sinensis*); but if you have a sunny window in a cool basement, an enclosed porch where temperatures do not drop to freezing, or an unheated guest room, then you can winter a Chinese hibiscus successfully. Ideal temperature should be 50° F. In the greenhouse it is possible to flower them at any time of the year, but their normal flowering period is summer and fall. During the winter they should be allowed to rest and the soil kept fairly dry with only occasional watering. In March repot in good, all-purpose potting soil and cut back the branches to about half their length. When growth resumes, keep the soil evenly moist and begin feeding with a plant food high in phosphorus. They require humidity of at least 50 percent; keep a water-filled pebble tray under plant and mist often. Move outdoors when danger of frost is past.

JADEPLANT

I have been told jadeplants bloom but have not had one of mine do so. Is it true that they do?

It is unusual for a jadeplant (*Crassula argentea*) grown as a house plant to bloom. Grown outdoors in a warm climate they do bloom, but only when they are large, mature plants.

JERUSALEM CHERRY

I purchased a Jerusalem cherry last fall. It was covered with the bright orange cherries, but they have since fallen off,

and many of the leaves are yellowing. What can I do to bring my plant back to bloom? I have been advised by a friend to treat this plant as a short-lived color accent and to forget about it.

The advice given by your friend is the one most commonly heard in connection with Jerusalem cherry (*Solanum pseudocapsicum*). However, a long time ago I was stubborn enough to ignore this advice and I have a large, healthy ten-year-old plant covered with "cherries" to prove that the preponderance of thought of this subject is wrong.

My first plant (a gift from my husband) survived and rebloomed for some time before it succumbed. The next fall when these plants filled the florists' shops with color, I bought a new one from my local florist. I told him I had had the first one for a year and wished to hang on to this one. His reply was "In that case, let me repot it for you." Apparently, since this myth that they do not survive is prevalent, those sold are potted in worthless soil.

So the first step is to repot your plant, immediately, in the same size pot, but substituting good sterile potting soil. Add a handful of sand (if you can get it) or some vermiculite or perlite for drainage. You will need a reasonably cool (70° F. daytime, 60 at night) sunny spot for it. While it is small, a windowsill is ideal. In the summertime, it needs to be outdoors. If you are an apartment dweller, try to find an obliging friend with a backyard garden or terrace. It should, of course, be protected from midday sun and watered copiously during the hot summer weather. During the rest of the year it should be kept evenly moist. (In my bedroom my Jerusalem cherry is the bellwether that warns me if I have been absentminded about watering: when the leaves begin to droop, I rush to water it and all the woody plants.)

Feed it monthly with a houseplant fertilizer and mist it daily. When it is brought back into the house, examine the undersides of the tip leaves carefully for eggs of its major nemisis—whitefully. These may also mysteriously appear on the plant in early spring. The eggs will appear to be small ($1/16$ to $1/8$ inch) translucent elongated seeds. Just

There are almost a countless variety of orchids that may be grown as flowering house plants. This one, a paphiopedilum or lady's slippers, requires the same care as that needed by African violets and gloxinias. (McDonald/Mulligan)

prune these tips off and burn them or put them in the garbage. The pruning appears to be quite beneficial promoting bushiness in the plants.

I nearly lost my plant last year while I was on vacation. Someone had been hired to water my plants, but a grouping clustered in the high shade of a tree on the lawn apparently had been overlooked. Fortunately, there had finally been some heavy rainfall so that when I returned, I found the bare bones of my plant surmounting luxuriant new growth that was coming back from the base of the branches. I pruned out all the dead wood, and, although it did not flower last year, this summer it was a glory of white flowers, and is now abundantly bowed down with orange fruit.

OLEANDER

I acquired a tub-grown oleander this summer which I intend to winter over in the house. Can you tell me how to treat it so it will bloom next summer?

Oleanders can be successfully wintered over in the house providing you can keep them fairly cool, and in a sunny, fresh, humid atmosphere. Let the soil go dry between waterings during the winter and then water thoroughly.

When the plants start to come into growth again in the spring, increase watering and set out of doors as soon as danger of frost is past. When flower buds begin to open, remove the new shoots forming at the base of the flowers, otherwise these may keep the buds from opening.

Water copiously until the flowers have faded. Then prune the old growth back by two-thirds the length of the branches. Reduce watering though not drastically, until new growth starts. Resume heavy watering until it is time to bring the plants in.

If plants need repotting, this is done in the spring before they are set out of doors. Plants in large tubs should have the upper inch of soil carefully removed and replaced with new soil. Grown as outdoor shrubs in California and Florida, oleanders are tolerant of poor soil and drought conditions, but potted oleanders need a sandy loam with rotted manure, peat or compost added. Feed monthly from spring through fall with a houseplant food such as that used for African violets.

POINSETTIA

I kept last Christmas's poinsettia growing, put it outside this summer and brought it in before frost. Although it has grown appreciably and is a fine healthy plant, it did not bloom at Christmas. How can I make it bloom?

Poinsettias (*Euphorbia pulcherrima*) are what are known as short-day plants, as are Christmas cactus and chrysanthemums. Outdoors in the frost-free climates of southern California and Florida they grow shrublike and bloom freely. As indoor plants they will not set flower (the flowers, incidentally, are the little yellow centers—the colorful "flowers" are actually colored bracts or leaves) unless their days grow shorter as they do outdoors. The plants should be rested during the early summer and watered less. When they are brought indoors, they should have no artificial light. If you do not have a room where they can have total darkness from sundown to sunrise, try to provide it by some means. Some people put them in closets, some cover them with a black cloth. I have seen them growing and flowering nicely in offices where the lights are turned off when everyone goes home at five o'clock.

QUEEN'S TEARS

I have been given a bromeliad called Queen's tears as a gift. Can you tell me how to take care of it?

Queen's tears (*Billbergia nutans*) is one of the easiest bromeliads for the average house. It is tolerant of average temperatures and does not need a lot of light—an eastern or western window is just right, or a spot a few feet away from a southern exposure will do. Your bromeliad was probably in bloom when given to you, as most gift plants are. The blossom will last a long time. Keep the "vase" formed by the rosette of stiff leaves filled with water. Once a week, drain out the old water and refill it with fresh water. Mist the plant frequently but try to avoid wetting the flower.

While it is growing and blooming, the potting medium should be kept watered; but during the winter months it can be allowed to go dry between waterings. Feed it during spring and summer, but dilute plant food to half the strength recommended.

After blooming, the plant may live only a year or two, but by that time new plantlets will have formed around the base. Do not remove these when they are too young or they won't have enough root system to survive. When they are six months old they should be ready. Cut them off, retaining as much of the root system as possible. They need a very light potting medium since these are epiphytic plants, which means air plants. In nature they grow perched in the crooks of trees where organic material has collected, just as some orchids do. They need air around their roots so should be potted in loose material. Chopped osmunda fiber, shredded redwood or fir bark, or a mixture of bark and perlite, vermiculite, or unmilled spagnum moss with charcoal chips added are all suitable. The lower third of the pot should be filled with broken crocks or pebbles for fast drainage. Set the small plants so the base of the leaves is above the potting medium. While the plants are small, use regular plant food at half strength during spring and summer. When they are larger, change to a high phosphorus one, also used at half strength.

It is believed that sealing a bromeliad in a plastic bag with an apple for a few days will cause it to bloom. The apple gives off ethylene gas which is supposed to help set the blossom. Do this a few weeks before normal blooming time, which is late winter or early spring.

Queen's tears and the other *Billbergias* are the bromeliads best suited to growing on a slab of osmunda fiber or for making a bromeliad tree. Wrap the roots with sheets of sphagnum moss and wire the plants onto the osmunda or in the angles of a tree branch. Be sure to keep the bromeliad's vase filled and to mist the plants every day.

WAXPLANT

Some years ago I purchased a small waxplant; apparently it was little more than a rooted cutting. For a long time it did not seem to grow at all. It finally has grown into a nice full plant. Can I expect it to bloom and what can I do to encourage it? It is a variety with white edging on the leaves.

Your waxplant sounds like a *Hoya carnosa variegata*. These plants do bloom with clusters of waxy-looking, star-shaped, intensely fragrant, pink flowers with dark red centers. The blooms appear in summer. I assume you are growing this as a house plant. In Florida and southern California it can be grown as an outdoor vine.

I have had an experience similar to yours with my wax plant. It took forever to get moving and then, although it was a handsome hanging basket, it did not bloom. The secret for success with this plant is to give it as much sun as possible all year round, but keep it cool and on the dry side in winter—water it about as frequently as you would a cactus. Most authorities recommend a winter temperature of about 45° F., but my plant is in my bedroom and, although it is cool, the night temperature does not drop below 60.

In the early spring, begin to water it more freely and feed it once a month with a plant food high in phosphorus, such as an African violet plant food. When the weather warms up, move it outdoors where it will get sun most of the day. My hoya is potted in a humusy potting soil with added vermiculite and sand. A prepared African violet mix or a soilless mix would also be fine. It is also pot-bound which I feel is one of the major factors in producing flowers.

In the summer I hang my hoya on the limb of a cherry tree where it gets lots of sun but not high noonday sun. Each year it produces more and more blossoms all summer long. The stems on which flowers are borne will flower again next year so don't cut them off if they look somewhat twiggy.

Although I recommend summering most house plants (with the notable exception of gesneriads) out-of-doors if at all possible, I do not believe it is necessary in order to induce bloom since buds are on the plant before it goes out.

For best results, group smaller house plants in pebble humidity trays. Here a fancy-leaf rhizomatous begonia, an episcia and gloxinias grow in a multi-shelf fluorescent-light garden. (McDonald/Mulligan)

By-mail Sources for Plants, Supplies, and Equipment

Although local nurseries, shops, and garden centers carry a wide variety of plants and supplies needed for their care, one of the most exciting aspects of gardening is reading and dreaming over the catalogs of mail-order specialists. These offer a ready, convenient source for virtually every plant in cultivation, plus highly specialized tools, equipment, and supplies.

The list that follows is by no means all-inclusive; inclusion is no more an endorsement than exclusion is condemnation. Over the years I have purchased plants and other materials from most of these firms and have almost always been pleased. I have also had the pleasure of visiting many of the nurseries and greenhouses listed, an experience I highly recommend.

Abbey Gardens, 176 Toro Canyon Rd., Carpinteria, Calif. 93013. Cacti and other succulents; 50¢ for catalog.

Abbot's Nursery, Rt. 4, Box 482, Mobile, Ala. 36609 Camellias.

Alberts & Merkel Brothers, Inc. 2210 S. Federal Highway, Boynton Beach, Fla. 33435. Orchids, tropical foliage, and flowering plants; 25¢ for list.

Antonelli Brothers, 2545 Capitola Rd., Santa Cruz, Calif. 95060. Tuberous begonias, gloxinias, archimenes.

Louise Barnaby, 12178 Highview St., Vicksburg, Mich. 49097. African violets; send stamp for list.

Mrs. Mary V. Boose, 9 Turney Pl., Trumbull, Conn. 06611. African violets and episcias; 15¢ for list.

John Brudy's Rare Plant House, P. O. Box 1348, Cocoa Beach, Fla. 32931. Unusual seeds and plants; $1 for catalog.

Buell's Greenhouses, Weeks Rd., Eastford, Conn. 06242. Complete listing of gloxinias, African violets, and other gesneriads; supplies; $1 for catalog.

Burgess Seed and Plant Co., 67 E. Battle Creek, Galesburg, Mich. 49053. Plants, bulbs, seeds.

W. Atlee Burpee Co., Warminster, Pa. 18974. Seeds, bulbs, plants; supplies.

David Buttram, P. O. Box 193, Independence, Mo. 64051. African violets; 10¢ for list.

Cactus Gem Nursery, 10092 Mann Dr., Cupertino, Calif. (visit Thursday–Sunday); by mail write P. O. Box 327, Aromas, Calif. 95004.

Carobil Farm & Greenhouses, Brunswick, Maine 04011. Catalog of geraniums.

Castle Violets, 614 Castle Rd., Colorado Springs, Colo. 80804. African violets.

Champion's African Violets, 8848 Van Hoesen Rd., Clay, N.Y. 13041. African violets; send stamp for list.

William Collier Orchids, Tissue Culture Laboratories, 6701 Cahuilla, Riverside, Calif. 92509

Cook's Geranium Nursery, 714 N. Grand, Lyons, Kans. 67544. Geraniums; 25¢ for catalog.

DeGiorgio Co., Inc. Council Bluffs, Iowa 51504. Seeds and bulbs.

P. De Jager and Sons, 188 Asbury St., South Hamilton, Mass. 01982. Bulbs.

L. Easterbrook Greenhouses, 10 Craig St., Butler, Ohio 44822. African violets, other gesneriads, terrarium plants; supplies; 75¢ for catalog.

Electric Farm, 104 B. Lee Rd., Oak Hill, N.Y. 12460. Gesneriads; send self-addressed stamped envelope for list.

Farmer Seed and Nursery Co., Faribault, Minn. 55021. Seeds, bulbs, plants.

Fennell Orchid Co., Inc. 26715 S.W. 157th Ave. Homestead, Fla. 33030. Orchids; supplies.

Fernwood Plants, 1311 Fernwood Pacific Dr., Topanga, Calif. 90290. Rare and unusual cacti.

Ffoulkes, 610 Bryan St., Jacksonville, Fla. 32202. African violets; 25¢ for list.

Henry Field Seed & Nursery Co., 407 Sycamore, Shenandoah, Iowa 51601. Plants, bulb, seeds; supplies.

Fischer Greenhouses, Linwood, N.J. 08221. African violets and other gesneriads; 25¢ for catalog.

Fox Orchids, 6615 W. Markham, Little Rock, Ark. 72205. Orchids, supplies.

Arthur Freed Orchids, Inc. 5731 S. Bonsall Dr., Malibu, Calif. 90255. Orchids; supplies.

J. Howard French, P. O. Box 87, Center Rutland, Vt. 05736. Bulbs.

French's Bulb Importer, P. O. Box 87, Center Rutland, Vt., 05736.

Golden Plant Nurseries, Inc., 7300 Astro St., Orlando, Fla. 32807.

Girard Nurseries, P. O. Box 428, Geneva, Ohio 44041. Bonsai materials.

Grigsby Cactus Gardens, 2354 Bella Vista Dr., Vista, Calif. 92083. Cacti and other succulents; 50¢ for catalog.

Gurney Seed and Nursery Co., Yankton, S.D. 57078. Seeds, bulbs, plants.

Orchids by Hausermann, Inc. P. O. Box 363, Elmhurst, Ill. 60126. Orchids; supplies; $1.25 for catalog.

Helen's Cactus, 2205 Mirasol, Brownsville, Tex. 78520. Cacti and other succulents; 10¢ for list.

Henrietta's Nursery, 1345 N. Brawley Ave., Fresno, Calif. 93704. Cacti and other succulents; 20¢ for catalog.

Hilltop Farm, Rte. 3, Box 216, Cleveland, Tex. Geraniums and herbs.

Sim T. Holmes, 100 Tustarawas Rd., Beaver, Pa. 15009. African violets, miniatures and regular.

Spencer M. Howard Orchid Imports, 11802 Huston St., North Hollywood, Calif. 91607. Unusual orchids.

Gordon M. Hoyt Orchids, Seattle Heights, Wash. 98036. Orchids; supplies.

Margaret Ilgenritz Orchids, Blossom Lane, P. O. Box 665, Monroe, Mich. Orchids; supplies; $1 for catalog.

Jones and Scully, 2200 N. W. 33rd Ave., Miami, Fla. 33142. Orchids and supplies; $3.50 for catalog.

K & L Cactus Nursery, 12712 Stockton Blvd., Galt, Calif. 95632.

Kartuz Greenhouses, 92 Chestnut St., Wilmington, Mass. Gesneriads, begonias, house plants.

Kirkpatrick's, 27785 De Anza St., Barstow, Calif. 92311. Cacti and other succulents; 10¢ for list.

Kolb's Greenhouses, 724 Belvedere Rd., Phillipsburg, N.J. 08865. African violets; and send stamp for list.

Lauray, Undermountain Road, Rte. 41, Salisbury, Conn. 06068. Gesneriads, cacti and other succulents, begonias; 50¢ for catalog.

Logee's Greenhouses, 55 North St., Danielson, Conn. 06239. Complete selection of house plants, with special emphasis on begonias and geraniums; $1 for catalog.

Paul Lowe, Mt. Vernon Springs, N.C. 27345. Begonias; 25¢ for catalog.

Lyndon Lyon, 14 Mutchler St., Dolgeville, N.Y. 13329. African violets and other gesneriads.

Mary's African Violets, 19788 San Juan, Detroit, Mich. 48221. African violets; supplies.

Earl May Seed & Nursery Company, Shenandoah, Iowa 51603. Seeds, bulbs, plants.

Rod McLellan Co., 1450 El Camino Real, South San Francisco, Calif. 94080. Orchids; supplies.

Merry Gardens, Camden, Maine 04843. House plants and herbs; large selection of begonias and geraniums; $1 for catalog.

Mini-Roses, P. O. Box 245, Station A, Dallas, Tex. 75208. Miniature roses.

Modlin's Cactus Gardens, Rte. 4, Box 3034, Vista, Calif. 92083. Cacti and other succulents; 25¢ for catalog.

Cactus by Mueller, 10411 Rosedale Highway, Bakersfield, Calif. 91001. Hybrid camellias and azaleas.

Orinda Nursery, Bridgeville, Del. 19933. Hybrid camellias.

George W. Park Seed Co., Inc., Greenwood, S.C. 29647. Seeds, bulbs, plants; supplies.

Penn Valley Orchids, 239 Old Gulph Rd., Wynnewood, Pa. 19096. Orchids.

Rainbox Begonia Gardens, P. O. Box 991, Westminister, Calif. 92683.

Routh's Greenhouse, Louisburg, Mo. 65685.

John Scheepers, Inc., 63 Wall St., N.Y. 10005. Flowering bulbs.

Sequoia Nursery, 2519 E. Noble St., Visalia, Calif. 93277. Miniature roses.

Shadow Lawn Nursery, 637 Holly Lane, Plantation, Fla. 33317. Seeds and cuttings; 50¢ for catalog.

Shaffer's Tropical Gardens, Inc., 3220 41 Ave., Capitola, Calif. 95010. Orchids.

P. R. Sharp, 104 N. Chapel Ave., #3 Alhambra, Calif. 91801. South American and Mexican cacti.

R. H. Shumway Seedsman, Rockford, Ill. 61101. Seeds, plants, bulbs.

Singers' Growing Things, 6385 Enfield Ave., Reseda, Calif. 90723. Cacti and other succulents; 30¢ for list.

Small World Miniature Roses, P. O. Box 562, Rogue River, Ore. 97537.

Fred A. Stewart, Inc., Orchids, 1212 East Las Tunas Dr., San Gabriel, Calif. 91778. Orchids; supplies.

Stokes Seeds, 737 Main St., Buffalo, N.Y. 14203.

Ed Storms, 4223 Pershing, Fort Worth, Tex. 76107. Lithops and other succulents.

Sunnybrook Farms, 9448 Mayfield Rd., Chestlerand, Ohio 44026. Herbs, scented geraniums, many other plants.

Sunnyslope Gardens, 8638 Huntington Dr., San Gabriel, Calif. 91775. Chrysanthemums.

Thompson & Morgan, Inc., P. O. Box 24, Somerdale, N.J. 08083. Seeds of many unusual plants.

Thon's Garden Mums, 4815 Oak St., Crystal Lake, Ill. 60014. Chrysanthemums.

Tinari Greenhouses, Box 190, 2325 Valley Rd., Huntingdon Valley, Pa. 19006. African violets, gesneriads; supplies; 25¢ for catalog.

Walther's Exotic House Plants, R. D. #3 Box 30, Catskill, N.Y. 12414.

White Flower Farm, Litchfield, Conn. 06759. Spectacular English hybrid tuberous-rooted begonias; other plants and bulbs.

Wilson Brothers, Roachdale, Ind. 47121. House plants, with special emphasis on geraniums.

Index

217

219